Louisiana Department of Education

The Public School Laws

Codified by Order of the State Board of Education

Louisiana Department of Education

The Public School Laws
Codified by Order of the State Board of Education

ISBN/EAN: 9783744666909

Printed in Europe, USA, Canada, Australia, Japan

Cover: Foto ©Suzi / pixelio.de

More available books at **www.hansebooks.com**

STATE OF LOUISIANA.
Department of Education.

THE

PUBLIC SCHOOL LAWS,

CODIFIED BY ORDER OF THE

STATE BOARD OF EDUCATION.

THIRD COMPILATION,

EDITED AND PUBLISHED BY

THE STATE SUPERINTENDENT OF PUBLIC EDUCATION,

BATON ROUGE:
THE ADVOCATE, OFFICIAL JOURNAL OF THE STATE OF LOUISIANA.
1894.

NOTE.

This book is public property, and is prepared for the use of school officers and teachers.

INTRODUCTORY.

A resolution by the State Board of Education, directing the preparation of this edition of the School Law, makes the work authoritative as a guide for school officers. For this reason it is deemed unnecessary to encumber the book with specific references to the sources from which it was compiled, such references appearing only in the preceding summary or syllabus of each general division of contents. The compiler sought to arrange the matter for the convenience of school officers, without regard to the order in which it is printed in legislative documents.

It is believed that this compilation contains all the constitutional and statutory provisions governing the school system of the State. It embraces general provisions relating to the public schools and the requirements for officers, many enactments providing a revenue, the lands appropriated for the use of public schools, and State educational institutions. Only the provisions for current revenue, acts of a local character, and repealing clauses have been omitted.

In the appendices may be found extracts from the decisions of the Supreme Court of Louisiana and regulations adopted by the State Board of Education.

The compiler has added a few annotations where experience has taught him to anticipate difficulties in construction.

A. D. LAFARGUE,
State Superintendent of Public Education.

CONSTITUTIONAL PROVISIONS.

(ADOPTED IN 1879.)

ART. 51. [Prohibiting State Aid to Sectarian Institutions.]— No money shall ever be taken from the public treasury, directly or indirectly, in aid of any church, sect or denomination of religion, or in aid of any priest, preacher, minister or teacher thereof, as such; and no preference shall ever be given to, nor any distinction made against any church, sect or creed of religion, or any form of religious faith or worship; nor shall any appropriations be made for charitable or benevolent purposes to any person or community; provided, this shall not apply to the State Asylums for the insane, and deaf, dumb and blind, and the charity hospitals and public charitable institutions conducted under State authority.

ART. 207. [Exemption of Educational Institutions from Taxation.]—The following property shall be exempt from taxation, and no· other, viz: All public property, places of religious worship or burial, all charitable institutions, all buildings and property used exclusively for colleges, or other school purposes, the real and personal estate of any public library and that of any other literary association, used by or connected with such library; all books and philosophical apparatus, and all paintings and statuary of any company or association kept in a public hall; provided, the property so exempted be not used or leased for purpose of private or corporate profit or income. There shall also be exempt from taxation household property to the value of five hundred dollars; there shall also be exempt from taxation and license for a period of twenty years from the adoption of the Constitution of 1879, the capital, machinery and other property employed in the manufacture of textile fabrics, leather, shoes, harness, saddlery, hats, flour, machinery, agricultural implements, manufacture of ice, fertilizers and chemicals, and furniture and other articles of wood, marble, or stone, soap, stationery, ink and paper, boat building and chocolate; provided, that not less than five hands are employed in any one factory.

ART. 208. [Poll Tax.]—The General Assembly shall levy an annual poll-tax for the maintainance of public schools, upon every male inhabitant in the State, over the age of twenty-one years, which shall never be less than one dollar, nor exceed one dollar and a half per capita, and the General Assembly shall pass laws to enforce payment of said tax.   *   *   *   *

ART. 224. [State School Tax.]—There shall be free public schools established by the General Assembly throughout the State, for the education of all the children of the State between the ages of six and eighteen years; and the General Assembly shall provide for their establishment, maintainance and support, by taxation or otherwise, and all moneys so raised, except the poll tax, shall be distributed to each parish in proportion to the number of children between the ages of six and eighteen years.

ART. 225. [State and Parish Superintendents.]—There shall be elected by the qualified voters of the State, a Superintendent of Public Education, who shall hold his office for the term of four years, and until his successor is qualified. His duties shall be prescribed by law, and he shall receive an annual salary of two thousand dollars.

The aggregate annual expenses of his office, including his salary, shall not exceed the sum of three thousand dollars. The General Assembly shall provide for the appointment of parish boards of public education for the different parishes.

The parish boards may appoint a parish superintendent of public schools in their respective parishes, who shall be ex-officio secretary of the parish board, and whose salary for his double functions shall not exceed two hundred dollars annually, except that in the parish of Orleans the salary of the parish superintendent shall be fixed by the General Assembly, to be paid out of the public school funds according to each parish respectively.

ART. 226. [Instruction in the French Language.]—The general exercises in the public schools shall be conducted in the English language, and the elementary branches taught therein; provided, that these elementary branches may be also taught in the French language in those parishes in the State, or localities in said parish, where the French language predominates, if no additional expense is incurred thereby.

ART. 227. [Poll Tax Applicable Exclusively to the Parish from which it is Collected.]—The funds derived from the collection of the poll-tax shall be applied exclusively to the maintenance of the public schools as organized under this constitution, and shall be applied exclusively to the support of the public schools in the parish in which the same shall be collected, and shall be accounted for and paid by the collecting officers directly to the competent school authorities of each parish.

SEC. 228. [Sectarian Schools Cannot Receive Public School Funds.]—No funds raised for the support of the public schools shall be appropriated for or used for the support of any sectarian schools.

ART. 229. [School Funds—Of What They Shall Consist.]—The school funds of this State shall consist of:

1. The proceeds of taxation for school purposes, as provided in the constitution.

2. The interest on the proceeds of all public lands heretofore granted by the United States for the use and support of the public schools.

3. Of all lands and other property which may hereafter be bequeathed, granted or donated to the State, or generally for school purposes.

4. All funds or property, other than unimproved lands, bequeathed or granted to the State, not designated for other purposes.

5. The proceeds of vacant estates falling under the law to the State of Louisiana.

The legislature may appropriate to the same fund the proceeds, in whole or in part, of public lands not designated for any other purposes, and shall provide that every parish may levy a tax for the public schools therein, which shall not exceed the State tax; provided, that with such tax the whole amount of parish taxes shall not exceed the limits of parish taxation fixed by this constitution.

ART. 230. [State University.]—The University of Louisiana, as at present established and located at New Orleans, is hereby recognized in its three departments—to-wit: the law, the medical and the agricultural departments—to be governed and controlled by appropriate faculties. The General Assembly shall, from time to time, make such provision for the proper government, maintenance and support of said State University of Louisiana, and all the departments thereof, as the public necessity and wellbeing of the people of the State of Louisiana may require, not to exceed ten thousand dollars annually.

The Louisiana State University and Agricultural and Mechanical College, now established and located in the city of Baton Rouge, is hereby recognized, and all revenues derived and to be derived from the sales of land or land scrip, donated by the United States to the State of Louisiana for the use of seminary of learning, and mechanical and agricultural college, shall be appropriated exclusively to the maintenance and support of said University and Mechanical and Agricultural College, and the General Assembly shall from time to time make such additional appropriations for the maintenance and support of said Louisiana State University and Agricultural and Mechanical College as the public necessities and the well-being of the people of the State of Louisiana may require, not to exceed ten thousand dollars annually.

ART. 231. [Colored University.]—The General Assembly shall also establish in the city of New Orleans a University for the education of persons of color, provide for its proper government, and shall make an annual appropriation of not less than five thousand dollars, nor more than ten thousand dollars for its maintenance and support.

ART. 232. [**Women Eligible to School Offices.**]—Women over twenty-one years of age shall be eligible to any office of control or management under the school laws of this State.

ART. 233. [**Free School Fund, Seminary Fund, and Agricultural and Mechanical College Fund.**]—The debt due by the State to the free school fund is hereby declared to be the sum of one million, one hundred and thirty thousand, eight hundred and sixty-seven 51-100 dollars in principal, and shall be placed on the books of the Auditor to the credit of the several townships entitled to the same; the said principal being the proceeds of the sales of land heretofore granted by the United States for the use and support of free public schools, which amount shall be held by the State as a loan, and shall be held and remain a perpetual fund, on which the State shall pay an annual interest of four per cent, from the first day of January, 1880, and that said interest shall be paid on the several townships in the State, entitled to the same in accordance with the act of Congress, No. 68, approved February 5, 1843; and the bonds of the State heretofore issued belonging to said fund, and sold under the act of the General Assembly, No. 81, of 1872, are hereby declared null and void, and the General Assembly shall make no provision for their payment, and may cause them to be destroyed.

The debt due by the State to the Seminary fund is hereby declared to be one hundred and thirty-six thousand dollars, being the proceeds of the sales of the land heretofore granted by the United States to the State, for the use of a Seminary of Learning, and said amount shall be placed to the credit of said fund on the books of the Auditor of the State, as a perpetual loan, and the State shall pay an annual interest of four per cent on said amount from January 1st, 1880, for the use of said Seminary of Learning ; and the consolidated bonds of the State now held for the use of said fund shall be null and void after the first day of January, 1880, and the General Assembly shall never make any provision for their payment, and they shall be destroyed in such manner as the General Assembly may direct.

The debt due by the State to the Agricultural and Mechanical College fund is hereby declared to be the sum of one hundred and eighty-two thousand, three hundred and thirteen 3-100 dollars, being the proceeds of the sales of lands and land scrip heretofore granted by the United States to this State, for the use of a College for the benefit of agriculture and mechanic arts; said amounts shall be placed .to the credit of said fund on the books of the Auditor and Treasurer of the State, as a perpetual loan, and the State shall pay an annual interest of five per cent on said amount from January 1st, 1880, for the use of said Agricultural and Mechanical College. The consolidated bonds of the State now held by the State for the use of said fund, shall be null and void after the first day of January, 1880, and the General Assembly shall not make any provision for their payment, and they shall be destroyed in such manner as the General Assembly may direct.

The interest provided for by this article shall be paid out of any tax that may be levied and collected for the general purposes of public education.

I. GENERAL PROVISIONS.

1. [S. 1, A. 81, 1888.]—State Board of Education; of whom composed and how appointed; a body corporate; compensation.

2. [S. 2, A. 81, 1888.]—Regular and called meetings.

3. [S. 4, A. 81, 1888.]—May require additional reports to be made by the parish superintendent.

4. [S. 3, A. 81, 1888.]—Appoints parish school directors; prepares rules for the government of the schools; adopts text-books.

5. [S. 1, A. 57, 1892.]—Women are eligible to school offices.

6. [S. 1, A, 29, 1892.]—Parish officers; term of office; how vacancies shall be filled; oath of office.

7. [Same.]—Removal for neglect of duty.

8. [S. 6, A. 81, 1888.]—Parish boards bodies corporate.

9. [S. 2, A. 70, 1882.]—Evidences of debt are non-negotiable.

10. [S. 4, A 82, 1873.]—State and parish boards cannot be compelled to give bond and security in suits.

I. General Provisions—Continued.

11. [*S.* 7, *A.* 122, 1874.]—Attorneys may be appointed to protect school interests.

12. [*S.* 9, *A.* 81, 1888.]—Attorney of the parish boards.

13. [*S.* 7, *A.* 81, 1888.]—Parish school boards; officers and auxiliary visiting trustees; must report all deficiences in the schools or neglect of duty to the State Board of Education; apportion the school fund, determine number and location of schools to be established, number of teachers to be employed and salaries; make rules for their own government; date of meetings; compensation; must exercise vigilance in securing all funds due; may receive land grants and provide for the erection of school houses; furniture, apparatus, contracts; change of school location.

14. [*S.* 73, *A.* 81, 1888]—Restrictions on contracts and debts

15. [*S.* 15, *A.* 81, 1888.]—President of the parish board: presides at . meetings of the board; calls special meetings; assists the parish superintendent, and signs contracts. Secretary: keeps a record of the board's proceedings.

16. [*S.* 1, *A.* 36, 1894.]—Reports to be made by certain officers to the

State Auditor.

17. [*S.* 2, *A.* 36, 1894.]—Reports to clerk of court.

18. [*S.* 3, *A.* 36, 1894.]—Salary not to be paid until the two foregoing sections are complied with.

19. [*S.* 1298, *R. S.* 1869.]—Power of the school boards with reference to expropriations.

20. [*S.* 1299, *R. S.* 1869.]—Institution of suit upon dissatisfaction at assessments.

21. [*S.* 1300, *R. S.* 1869]—Failure of officers to perform duty imposed.

22. [*S* 1305, *R. S.* 1869.]—The sale which can be made by the Register of the Land Office.

23. *S* 1306, *R. S.* 1869.]—How located.

24. [*S.* 1307, *R. S.* 1869.]—Reservations of school lands.

25. [*S.* 1308, *R. S.* 1869.]—Scrips should issue only when locations cannot be made.

26. [*S.* 2, *A.* 89, 1894. —Exemptions from jury duty.

27. *S* 11, *A.* 81, 1888.] - Division of parishes into school districts.

28 [*S.* 12, *A.* 81, 1888.]—School districts in two adjoining parishes; how laid off.

29. [*S.* 13, *A.* 81, 1888.]—Option when school districts adjoin as to which school certain children will attend.

Section 1. [State Board of Education.]—The Governor and the Superintendent of Public Education, and the Attorney General, together with six citizens to be appointed by the Governor, one from each Congressional District of the State, shall be a body politic and corporate by the name and style of the Board of Education for the State of Louisiana, with authority to sue and defend suits in all matters relating to the interest of the public schools. The above spectfied six citizens shall receive, as compensation for their services in attending the meetings of the board, their actual traveling expenses and *per diem* for the number of days that the board is in session, the same as members of the State Legislature, payable on their warrants, approved by the president and secretary of the board, out of the school fund.

SEC. 2. [Time of Meeting.]—The Governor shall be *ex-officio* the president, and the State Superintendent the secretary. The board shall meet on or before the first Monday of December of each year, and at other times upon the call of the State Superintendent. , The acts of the board shall be attested by the signature of the president.

SEC. 3. [May Require Reports of Parish Superintendents.]— The State Board of Education may require reports to be made by the parish superintendent whenever the interest of the common schools indicate the necessity of other reports than now required.

SEC. 4. [Duties and Powers; Appoint School Directors; Text Books.]—The State Board of Education shall appoint for each parish in the State, except the parish of Orleans, a board of school directors consisting of not less than five, nor more than nine, qualified citizens of the parish. The Governor shall issue a commission to each of said directors. The State Board of Education shall prepare rules, by-laws and regulations for the government of the common schools of the State, which shall be enforced by the parish superintendents and the several school boards, and shall give such directions as it may see proper as to the branches of study which shall be taught. The State Board shall strictly enforce a uniformity of text books in all the public schools, and shall adopt a list thereof, which shall remain unchanged for four years after such adoption. For satisfactory reasons shown to said board, it may change said list or adopt a list generally preferred by teachers or parents in certain localities, maintaining as far as possible a uniformity of text books, and without placing parents and guardians to further expense. The adoption of such a list and apparatus shall be by contract to the lowest bidder, subject to the change aforesaid, and to the best advantage as to cost to pupils.

SEC. 5. [**Women Eligible to Office.**]—Article 233 of the Constitution of 1879 of the State of Louisiana is hereby declared to be operative, and women over twenty-one years of age are hereby declared eligible to any office of control or management under the School Laws of this State.

SEC. 6 |**Term of Office; Parish Officers.**]—The term of office of the members of the school boards and of the parish superintendents shall be four years from the time of their appointment. All vacancies occurring on the parish school boards during the interval between the meetings of the State Board of Education shall be filled by appointment by the Governor subject to the ratification of said Stat· board at its next meeting; provided these officers of the parish boards shall take the usual oath of office, which oath shall be filed in the office of the State Superintendent of Public Education.

SEC. 7. [**Removal for Neglect of Duty or Malfeasance in Office.**] —For neglect of duty or malfeasance in office the Governor may remove a member or members of this parish boards of school directors subject to the ratification of the State Board of Education; and for sufficient cause the parish board ot school directors may remove the parish superintendent of public education, subject to an appeal to the State Board of Education; provided, this appeal be taken within ten days after his dismissal. The appeal shall not have the effect of suspending the board's action of dismissal during its pendency but the parish superintendent shall be reinstated if the State board decides that he was dismissed without cause and reverses the decision of the parish school board.

SEC. 8. [**School Boards Bodies Corporate.**]—The several school boards are constituted bodies corporate with power to sue and be sued, under the name and style of the "Parish Board of

Directors of the Parish of ———," as the case may be. Citations shall be served on the president of the board.

SEC. 9. [**Evidences of Debt Not Negotiable.**]—Said board shall have no power to issue negotiable evidences of debt.

SEC. 10. [**State and Parish Boards Exempt from Furnishing Bonds in Suit.**—In all judicial proceedings where, by law, bond and security are required from litigants, the State Board of Education shall be dispensed from furnishing bond or security; and in all suits in which the State or parish board of education may be plaintiffs, defendants, intervenors, garnishees, or interested in any manner whatsoever, it shall be the duty of the court-before whom such suits are pending, on the affidavit of the attorney representing the State or parish board of education, if the case is one of serious public interest and in which a speedy decision is desirable, to set the cause for trial by preference, and all such cases may also be fixed for trial as early as possible on motion or petition of the attorney of the State or parish board of education.

SEC. 11. [**State Superintendent to Appoint Attorneys in Certain Cases.**]—The Superintendent of Public Education may appoint a person of legal attainments in each school division (parish) of the State, to examine notes due and other assets arising out of purchase of lands granted to educational purposes; to recover lands improperly held and revenues diverted, and generally protect the school interests in matters appertaining thereto. He (the attorney) shall be paid a commission on moneys recovered, not exceeding ten per cent, and on the value of lands and other property recovered, not exceeding five per cent.

SEC. 12. [**Attorney of Parish Board.**]—The district attorney of the district, or any other attorny selected by the board, shall act as counsel for the parish board.

SEC. 13 [**Duty and Authority of Parish Boards.**]—The parish board of directors shall select from their number a president. They shall elect or appoint a parish superintendent, who shall be ex-officio secretary of the board. They are authorized, in their discretion, to appoint auxiliary visiting trustees for each ward or school district, or school in the parish; such trustees to make quarterly reports to the parish boards of the actual condition of, and shall make needful suggestions in all matters relating to the schools they have in charge as trustees. The parish board of directors shall report to the State Board of Education all deficiencies in the schools, or neglect of duty on the part of teachers, superintendent or other officer. They shall visit and examine the schools in the several school districts of the parish, from time to time, and they shall meet and advise with the trustees when occasion requires (if auxiliary trustees be appointed by the board of the parish). They shall apportion the school fund to the several districts in the parish in proportion to the number of persons in the district between the ages of six and eighteen years, and shall determine the number of schools to be opened, the location of the school houses, the number of teachers to be employed, their salary; and the said school board is entrusted with seeing that the provisions of the law are complied with. They shall make such rules and by-laws for their own government (not inconsistent with the law) as they may deem proper. The regular meeting of each parish board shall be held on the first Saturday of January, April, July and October, and it may hold such special and adjourned meetings as the board may determine, or as occasion may require. Each member shall receive payment for his attendance at school board meetings, when the board shall hold regular sessions on the days before mentioned; provided, that the amount be not fixed by the said board at more than two dollars per diem, and provided that the whole amount expended annually shall not exceed one hundred dollars. The school boards shall exercise proper vigilance in securing for the schools of the parish all funds destined for the support of the schools, including the State fund apportioned thereto, the poll tax collectible, and all other funds. They shall keep a record of all their transactions and proceedings. The school boards may receive land by purchase or donation, for the purpose of erecting a school house, provide for and secure the erection of same, construct such outbuildings and enclosures as shall be conducive to the protection of the property, make repairs and provide the necessary furniture and apparatus. All contracts for improvements shall be to the lowest responsible bidder, the board reserving the right to reject any and all bids. They shall have power to recover for any damages that may be done the property in their charge; they may, by a two-third vote of the whole board, after due notice, change the location of the school-house, sell or dispose of the old site and use the proceeds thereof towards procuring a new one.

SEC. 14. [Restrictions on Contracts and Debts.]—The different boards of directors shall not be empowered to make contracts or debts for any one year greater than the amount of revenue prov'ded for according to this act, it being the intent hereof that parties contracting with said board shall take heed that due revenue shall have been provided to satisfy the claim, otherwise they may lose and forfeit the same, and no action or execution shall be allowed in aid thereof, and that the board shall not exceed their powers in incurring the debt.

SEC. 15. [Duties of President and Secretary of the Board.]— The president shall preside at the meetings of the board, call special meetings when necessary, advise with and assist the parish superintendent in promoting the success of the schools, and generally do and perform all other acts and duties pertaining to his office of president of the board. All deeds and contracts for the schools, including those with teachers, are to be signed by him; the latter also by the parish superintendent.

The secretary shall keep full minutes of all proceedings of the board in a book provided for the purpose, and shall do and perform all other acts and duties legally pertaining to the office of secretary of the board.

SEC. 16. [Reports of State and Parish Boards and Officers.]— In addition to the biennial reports now required by law from State and district boards, the State and district officers, or other persons receiving or disbursing State or district funds,

said boards, officers and persons shall render, in writing, to the
State Auditor, semi-annual itemized detailed reports, which in
case of the report of a board or its representatives, shall be signed
by the president and secretary of the board, showing the several
sums received and from what source, and the several sums disbursed and for what purpose and to whom paid, the said reports
to be made on or before the first days of June or December of each
year; and in the event of the failure so to do on the part of any
board or district officer or other person above named, the Auditor
shall report the delinquency to the Governor within fifteen days
after said failure, who shall be authorized thereupon, to remove
from office the members of said board, or district officer or other
person as for cause, unless it may be made to appear to the satisfaction of the Governor, that said failure or delinquency occurred
from unavoidable or excusable causes.

SEC. 17.   [Concerning Officers.]—All parish boards and parish officers having in charge the reception of, or disbursement of, public funds shall make semi-annual itemized, detailed
accounts as required above to the clerk of court of the respective
parishes, under the forms, conditions and penalties enumerated
in Section 16 of this act.

SEC. 18.   [Penalties for Non-Compliance.]—In case any sala-
ried officer of the State failing to file with the Auditor of
Public Accounts semi-annual itemized, detailed accounts, as
provided in the sixteenth section of this act the Auditor shall,
within fifteen days thereafter, furnish to the Treasurer of the
State, a certificate to that effect and thereafter it shall be illegal
for the Auditor to audit any warrant of said officer for salary,
or the Treasurer to pay the same, until such time as the delinquent officer shall have complied with the foregoing provisions.

SEC. 19.   [Power of the District Board in Expropriations.]—
When land shall be required for the erection of a school house
or for enlarging a school house lot, and the owner refuses to
sell the same for a reasonable compensation, the District Board
of School Directors shall have the power to select and possess

such sites embracing space sufficiently extensive to answer the purpose of school house and grounds.

SEC. 20. [**Relative to the Value of the Grounds.**]—Should such land holder deem the sum assessed too small, he shall have the right to institute suit before any proper judicial tribunal for his claim; but the title shall pass from him to the school corporation.

SEC. 21. [**Penalty for Non-Performance of Duty.**]—A failure on the part of any district, parish or State officer to perform the duty imposed upon him by any section of this act, under the title, "Education," and in the manner herein specified, is hereby declared a misdemeanor in office. Upon conviction thereof, such officer shall be punished by a fine not less than fifty, and not exceeding one hundred dollars, and by imprisonment in the parish prison for a term of not less than thirty days, and not exceeding three months. All prosecutions for offenses against this section shall have precedence over all cases before any justice of the peace, parish or district court.

SEC. 22. [**Sale Which Can be Made by the Land Register.**]— It shall be lawful for the Register of the Land Office to sell, at the price stipulated by law, to any Board of Free School Directors of this State, any amount, not less than five acres, of any land within their school district, donated by Congress to this State, either for the use of a seminary of learning, or for the purpose of internal improvement, on which to erect a school house.

SEC. 23. [**How Located.**]—Any land so sold shall commence in the corner of a legal division or sub-divisions of sections; and if in a right angle, it shall be run an equal distance on two sides, bounded by the line of such division, and form a square including the number of acres sold; if in an acute angle, it shall be bounded by said division lines to such distance, and by lines in such other directions as the Register may deem most equitable between the land so sold and that retained; the patents for lands so sold shall issue to the free school directors and

2

their successors, for the use of their district schools, setting forth the number, and of what parish.

SEC. 24. [Reservations of School Lands.]—The Register of the State Land Office at Baton Rouge is required to ascertain in what township, in this State, there are no reservations of school sections' by reason of conflicting claims or from any other cause, or where the reservation is less than contemplated by law; and in such cases it is made his duty under the superintendence of the Governor, to apply for, and as soon as possible, obtain a location of any land or part of land in lieu thereof.

SEC. 25. [Scrips Should Issue Only When Locations Cannot be Made.]—When such locations cannot be made, if deemed more advantageous to the State, the Register, with the assent of the Federal Government, is authorized to issue scrip for such lands, which scrip shall not be sold for a less amount than one dollar and twenty-five cents per acre.

SEC. 26. [Exemptions from Jury Duty.]—The following persons shall be exempted from serving as jurors, but the exemption shall be personal to them, and when they do not themselves claim the exemption it shall not be sufficient cause from challenging any person exempt under the provisions of this act. * * * The Governor, Lieutenant Governor, State Auditor, State Treasurer, Secretary of the State, Superintendent of Public Education, their clerks and employees, and all public officers, commissioned under the authority of the United States. * * * professors and school teachers while employed in teaching. * * * * * * * * * *

SEC. 27. [Division of Parishes Into School Districts.]—It shall be the duty of the parish board, with the parish superintendent, to divide the parish into school districts of such proper and convenient area and shape as will best accommodate the children of the parish. The parish boards shall, as soon as practicable, proceed to the work imposed upon them, and upon completing this work, they shall make a report to the parish superintendent, which report shall contain the boundary and description of the said district designated by number. The parish superintendent shall record the same in a well bound book, kept by him for the purpose, which book shall be held by said parish superintendent, and be at all times open to inspection. The parish board, if they deem it to the best interests of the schools, may divide the parish into districts without reference to the wards in the parish.

SEC. 28. [School Districts in Two Adjoining Parishes; How Laid Off.]—The parish superintendents of two adjoining parishes, where the division line intersects a neighborhood whose convenience requires it, may lay off a district composed of parts of both the parishes. Such districts shall be reported, together with the census of school children only as belonging to the parish in which the school house may be situated, by the parish superintendent of the parish; and report shall be made by the assessor and the parish superintendent as though it lay entirely in the parish.

SEC. 29. [Option Which District School Children Will Attend.] Where two school districts adjoin, it shall be lawful for the children in either of the said adjoining districts to be taught in and at such school house as shall be most convenient to them; provided, that their tuition fees shall be paid to the district in which they are taught, and that no change be made without the assent of the school boards of the respective parishes.

II. State Superintendent of Public Education.

30. [S. 16, A. 81, 1888.]—An office to be provided for the State Superintendent; custody of papers and records; vacancy filled by appointment from the Governor.

31. [S. 17, A. 81, 1888]—Salary of the State Superintendent, his office, stationery, clerk, porter.

32. [S. 18, A. 81, 1888.]—Duties of the State Superintendent and the schools subject to his supervisory control

33. [S. 19, A 81, 1888]—Accounts he shall keep.

34. [S. 20, A. 81, 1888.]—Biennial report; what it shall contain; number of copies to be printed and distributed.

35. [S. 21, A. 81, 1888.]—Institutions

II. STATE SUPERINTENDENT OF PUBLIC EDUCATION—
Continued.

of the Blind and the Deaf and Dumb; Reports and suggestions to be made by the State Superintendent.

36. [*S.* 22, *A.* 81, 1888.]—Copies of the State Superintendent's records and papers admissible in evidence.

37. [*S.* 23, *A.* 81, 1888.]—Must report neglect of duty and the improper use of school funds.

38. [*S.* 24, *A.* 81, 1888.]—Decisions and appeals.

SEC. 30. [**State Superintendent of Public Education.**]—An office shall be provided for the State Superintendent of Public Education at the seat of government, in which he shall file, each year separately, all papers, reports and public documents transmitted to him by the board and officers whose duty it is to report to him, and hold the same in readiness to be examined by the Governor whenever he sees proper, and by any committee appointed by the General Assembly; and he shall cause to be kept a record of all matters appertaining to his office. In case of vacancy in the office of Superintendent of Public Education, the Governor shall fill the vacancy and submit the name of the appointee to the Senate for its confirmation at the first session held after the appointment.

SEC. 31. [**Salary, Office Expenses, Clerk, Porter.**]—The salary of the Superintendent of Public Education shall be two thousand dollars per annum, besides which he shall be entitled to office fixtures, stationery, books, fuel and lights needed to carry on the work of his office. He shall have the authority to appoint a clerk and a porter, and prescribe the duties of each; provided, that the entire expenses of his office, including salaries, postage and incidentals, shall not exceed the specific appropriation therefor, payable in monthly installments, out of the current school fund, by the Treasurer of the State, upon the warrants of the State Superintendent.

SEC. 32. [**Duties of the State Superintendent.**]—The State Superintendent of Public Education shall have general supervision of all boards of education, and of all common, high or normal schools of the State, and shall see that the school system is carried into effect properly. He shall visit the several parishes of the State whenever practicable, at least once a year, and shall give due notice of the time of his intended visit to the parish superintendent, whose duty it shall be to meet and confer with the State Superintendent on all matters connected with the interests of the common schools of the parish; while engaged in this duty, his actual expenses shall be paid out of the current school fund, but shall not in any case exceed the amount appropriated per annum for the purpose.

SEC. 33. |General Duties of the State Superintendent.]— He shall keep an account of all orders drawn or countersigned by him on the Auditor of all returns of settlements, and make note of all changes, in the appointment of school treasurers; whenever required any part of this account or note of change shall be furnished by the Auditor.

SEC. 34. [Biennial Report.]—He shall biennially, on or before the meeting of the General Assembly, make a report of the condition and progress made and possible improvements to be made in the common schools; the amount and condition of the school funds; how its revenues, during the two previous school years, have been distributed; the amount collected and disbursed for common school purposes from local taxation or from any other source of revenue, and how the same was expended. This report shall contain an abstract of the parish and city superintendents' reports. He shall communicate all facts, statistics and information as are of interest to the common schools. He shall cause to be printed a copy for each school district in the State, two hundred copies for the use of the members of the legislature, and to exchange with the superintendents of public instruction of other States, and three hundred copies for distribution by the superintendent.

SEC. 35. [Suggestions to be Made Concerning Institutions for the Blind, Deaf and Dumb.]—The Superintendent in his report shall set forth the objects, make suggestions which may be of interest and promote the success of the Institutions of the Blind and the Deaf and Dumb. The superintendents of these institutions shall annually, by the first day of March, furnish the State Superintendent of Public Education such statements of their respective institutions as may be necessary to enable him to make a full and satisfactory report.

SEC. 36. [Copies of Superintendent's Records Admissible in Evidence.]—Certified copies of records and papers in his office shall, in all cases, be evidence as admissible as the original.

SEC. 37. [Reports to State Board in Certain Cases.]—It is made part of his duty to report all neglect of duty or any improper uses made of school funds to the State Board of Education whenever it may come to his knowledge.

SEC. 38.* [Decisions and Appeals.]—The State Superintendent shall decide all controversies or disputes that may arise or exist among the directors, or between the superintendents and the board, and between the superintendents and teachers concerning their respective duties. The facts of these controversies or disputes shall be made known to him by written statements by the parties thereto, verified by oath or affirmation, if required, and accompanied by certified copies of all necessary minutes, contracts, orders or other documents. An appeal may be taken from his decision to the Board of Education, provided it be taken within fifteen days after his decision shall have been made· When called upon by the Superintendent of Public Education the Attorney General shall give his opinion in regard to any controversy or dispute. The Superintendent of Public Education shall, whenever required, give advice, explanations, constructions or informations to the district officers and superintendents and citizens relative to the common school law ; the duties of common school officers; the right and duties of parents,

---

*SECTION 38. This department will gladly assist in every way in securing uniform and satisfactory administration of school affairs. The custom of answering proper inquiries, from school officers, teachers or others, touching constructions and app ications of school laws, will continue. All correspondence of this kind is filed here for preservation, letter-press copi s being taken for that purpose. It is obvious that we cannot comply with requests for the return of letters of inquiry with our replies.

In appealing to the State Superintendent, copies of the charges verified by oath should be furnished the officers or persons complained against that they may answer for themselves.

guardians, pupils and all officers: the management of the schools, and all other questions calculated to promote the cause of education.

III. PARISH SUPERINTENDENT, TREASURER, AND OTHER OFFICERS.

39. [*S*. 25, *A*. 81, 1888.]—Qualifications and salary of the Parish Superintendent.

40. [*S*. 26, *A*. 81, 1888,]—Must visit each school once a year.

41. [*S*. 27, *A*. 81, 1888]—Additional compensation allowed for certain services.

42. [*S*. 28, *A*. 81, 1888.]—Committee for the selection of teachers.

43. [*S*. 29, *A*. 81, 1888.]—Enumeration of educable youth—each Parish Superintendent to forward an annual statement to the State Superintendent.

44. [*S*. 16, *A* 85, 1888.]—Duty of Assessor in enumerating youths.

45. [*S*. 30, *A*. 81, 1888]—Parish Superintendent to report annually to the State Superintendent.

46. [*S*. 31, *A*. 81, 1888.]—Custody of official documents by the Parish Superintendents.

47. [*S*. 32, *A*. 81, 1888.]—Oaths he may administer.

48. [*S*. 33, *A*. 81, 1888]—His office days.

49. [*S*. 56, *A*. 81, 1888]—Parish Treasurer is ex-officio School Treasurer.

50. [*S* 57, *A*. 81, 1888.]—His bond; in favor of the Governor; amount; certified copies must be furnished the State Superintendent and the State Treasurer.

51. [*S* 58, *A*. 81, 1888.]—Transfer of funds and documents of Parish Treasurer to his successor.

52. [*S* 59, *A*. 81, 1888.]—How funds shall be disbursed

53. [*S*. 60, *A*. 81, 1888.]—Parish Treasurer's compensation.

54. [*S*. 61, *A*. 81, 1888]—Receipts and disbursements by the Parish Treasurer; his report to the State Superintendent.

SEC. 39. [**Qualifications; Salary.**]—There shall be a parish superintendent in each of the parishes of the State, the parish of Orleans excepted, who shall be possessed of moral character and ability to manage the common school interest of the parish. He shall be of age. His salary shall not be more than two hundred dollars per annum for his services as superintendent and secretary as herein provided.

SEC. 40. [**Visits to be Made.**]—He shall during the year visit once, at least, each school district in the parish, and he shall exert his best endeavors in promoting the cause of common school education.

SEC. 41. [Additional Compensation.]—Whenever his services are quite efficient and highly satisfactory to the school board,
it is authorized in its discretion to allow an amount sufficient to
the parish superintendent to defray his expenses in visiting all
the schools in his parish. The amount allowed shall never
exceed one hundred and twenty-five dollars per annum. Prior
to any payment for expenses in visiting the schools, he shall
make a written report respecting the condition of each school
examined, and · shall make it appear that he has devoted at
least three hours in examining each school visited. The school
board is also authorized to defray his expenses to attend annually the convention of superintendents.

SEC. 42.* [Committee for Appointment of Teachers.]—The
president of the school board and a member appointed by the
board, also the parish superintendent, shall constitute a committee, and shall as such appoint the teachers of the common schools
for his parish, and fill vacancies in the order of merit as hereinafter provided. At the first meeting of the board after the
appointment, it shall be noted in each instance in the minutes of
its proceedings.

SEC. 43. [Enumeration of Educable Youth.]—It shall be the
duty of the parish superintendent, on or before the 10th day
of January of each year, to cause to be placed in the hands of
the State Superintendent of Public Education a report showing
the number of children between the ages of six and eighteen
years, residing in the parish, and the whole number residing in
each district designated by its number. He shall take the
items of his report from the assessor's returns showing the said
number of children, but he shall assure himself of its correctness, and so attest before a competent officer.

---

*SECTION 42. The contract thus resulting from the appointment of teachers by the appoint-
ment committee is binding upon the board and only annulled when its conditions are unfulfilled
and when it contains unauthorized terms as are solely determinable by the parish board, as
matters of school location, number of teachers employed, and salaries.

The superintendent may discharge teachers found unworthy of the trust confided to them.

For neglect of duty, the board may remove the parish superintendent.

The board must hold its executive officers responsible in such manner that arrangements
will have a positive character and shall not be liable to frequent and harmful changes.

SEC. 44. [Assessor's Enumeration.]—The assessors of the several parishes throughout the State (the parish of Orleans excepted,) shall furnish to the Auditor of Public Accounts, within the time prescribed by section 12 (the first of January of each year) with blank forms of assessments, as follows, viz:

* * * WHITE CHILDREN BETWEEN SIX AND EIGHTEEN YEARS.

MALES,
FEMALES,
COLORED CHILDREN BETWEEN SIX AND EIGHTEEN YEARS.
MALES,   •
FEMALES,

And it shall be the duty of the said assessors * * * to correctly return the * * statistics thereto attached.

SEC. 45. [Annual Report of Parish Superintendent.]—He (the parish superintendent) shall previously to the 15th day of January, mail to the State Superintendent of Public Education his official report, showing in tables an aggregate of the school districts in his parish by number, the districts in which schools were taught, and the length of time taught, the highest, the lowest, and the average number of children at school, the cost of tuition of each child for the session and per month, number of private schools, academies and colleges taught in the parish, and the length of session of same; the number of teachers employed, male and female, for the common schools, the average wages of male teachers, female teachers, the amount of money raised for school purposes in the parish by local tax or otherwise, and for whose purposes it was disbursed; the number and kind of school houses, and the value of each, the number built during the year preceding the report, the number of district libraries and the number of volumes in each, and the increase during the year, the amount received and expended. In case of his neglect or failure to make this report in time as required, he shall forfeit and pay the sum of twenty dollars of his annual salary.

SEC. 46. [Custody of Records, Papers, and Documents.]— Each parish superintendent shall keep a record of all the business transacted by him as parish superintendent, the names and numbers, and description of school districts, and all other papers and documents of value connected with his office, at all times subject to inspection and examination by any school officer or other person interested in any question pertaining to the common school.

SEC. 47. [Oaths Superintendent May Administer.]—The parish superintendent may administer the oath required of any of the officials of the common schools, or of any person required to make oath in any matter relating thereto, except to qualify directors.

SEC. 48. [Office Days.]—He shall attend at his office, at the parish seat, on the first Saturday of January, April, July and October, in each year, and at such other times as may be necessary for him to receive the reports of teachers and others, and to transact the business required of him.

SEC. 49. [Parish Treasurer is Ex-Officio School Treasurer.]— The parish treasurer in every parish (the parish of Orleans excepted) shall be and is constituted the treasurer of all school funds apportioned by the State to such parish, or raised, collected or donated therein for the support of the free public schools; he shall receive and receipt for all such funds to the Treasurer of the State, and to the collector of parish taxes.

SEC. 50. [Bond of the Treasurer.]—Immediately upon the passage of this act, and thereafter before he enters upon the duties of his office, the parish treasurer of each parish who shall be elected after the passage of this act, shall, in addition to the bond required by existing law, execute a bond in favor of the Governor of the State, with good and solvent security, in a sum equal to the amount annually apportioned to the parish; the sureties on said bond shall be residents of the parish, and shall own therein real estate worth over and above all incumbrance the amount of their obligations thereon; said bond must be accepted by the president of the board of directors, and the clerk of the district court, who shall record the same in the mortgage book of the parish, and shall forward to the State Superintendent of Education and to the State Treasury a copy of said bond, with a certificate of its acceptance and registry endorsed thereon.

SEC. 51. [**Transfer of Funds.**]—Said treasurer, immediately upon the acceptance of his bond, shall demand of his predecessor in the office of the treasurer of the school funds, the custody of all books and papers and of all balances of school money in his hand as custodian of the school funds of the parish.

SEC. 52. [**How Funds Shall be Disbursed.**]—Said treasurer shall pay out of the school funds intrusted to his charge only on warrants drawn by the president and countersigned by the secretary of the parish school board, and shall state against what school district fund it was drawn, which warrants shall be drawn by these officers only in virtue of appropriations regularly made by the parish board; the parish board shall make annually an estimate of the amount of revenue for the year, appropriating the same as above required, and no warrant beyond the amount estimated shall be drawn for any year. These warrants shall be numbered and shall specify on their face to whom and for what they are given, and the date of the appropriation made by the school board; the treasurer shall pay these warrants only to the extent of the amount to the credit on his books, and in the order in which they are presented, of school districts, in behalf of which the warrants shall have been drawn, and said warrants shall be filed in the office as vouchers, and with the account book kept by him as treasurer of the school fund shall always be subject to examination by any one who chooses to examine them.

SEC. 53. [**Treasurer's Compensation.**]—The compensation of the treasurer shall be a sum to be fixed by the State Board of Education, for each parish, according to its territorial area and the amount of fund to be disbursed; but in no case shall it exceed two and a half per cent of the amount disbursed by him as shown by his vouchers.

SEC. 54. [**Treasurer's Report.**]—It shall be the duty of the treasurer to furnish to the parish board accounts of his receipts and disbursements as often as required by them, and before the 10th day of January, annually he shall forward to the State Superintendent of Public Education, in such form as he shall prescribe, a full report of his receipts and disbursements for the year, and of the balance on hand to the credit of each ward or school district, and the indebtedness outstanding on the first day of January; provided, the foregoing sections do not apply to the treasurer of the board for the parish of Orleans.

IV. TEACHERS.

INSTITUTES.

55. [*S.* 34, *A.* 81, 1888.]—Date for parish institutes.

56. [*S.* 35, *A.* 81, 1888.]—Attendance at the parish institutes obligatory upon teachers; exceptions.

57. [*S.* 36, *A.* 81, 1888.]—Length of institute session; penalty for non-attendance.

58. [*S.* 37, *A.* 81, 1888.]—Members of the institute, active and honorary.

59. [*S.* 38, *A.* 31, 1888.]—Roll of institute members.

60. [*S.* 39, *A* 81, 1888]—Parish superintendents to appoint institute managers; manager's pay.

61. [*S.* 40, *A.* 81, 1888.]—Institute fund; superintendent's compensation for personal superintendence at institute.

62. [*S.* 41, *A.* 81, 1888]—Foregoing sections not applicable to Orleans parish.

63. [*S.* 43, *A.* 81, 1888.]—Institute report by parish superintendent

64. [*S* 1, *A.* 64, 1894]—State teachers' institutes

65. [*S.* 2, *A.* 64, 1894.] - State institute conductor; how elected; salary.

66. [*S.* 3, *A.* 64, 1894.]—State institute conductor, an ex-officio

member of the State Normal School faculty.

67. [*S.* 4, *A.* 64, 1894.]—Assistant institute lecturers; remuneration.

68. [*S.* 5, *A.* 64, 1894]—State Superintendent and the President of the Normal School ex-officio State institute managers.

69. [*S.* 6, *A.* 64, 1894]—Local arrangements for institutes; notification to teachers to attend institutes.

70. [*S.* 7, *A.* 64, 1894.]—Penalty for inexcusable absence of teachers from institutes.

71. [*S.* 8, *A* 64, 1894.]—Leaves of absence to be granted and salaries continued.

72. [*S.* 9, *A.* 64. 1894.]—Certificates of attendance.

73. [*S.* 10, *A.* 64, 1894.]—Report of the institute conductor.

EXAMINATIONS.

74. [*S.* 44, *A.* 81, 1888.]—When two or more teachers apply for the same position, it shall be awarded by competitive examination.

75. [*S.* 45, *A.* 81, 1888.]—Examination fee.

76 [*S.* 46, *A.* 81, 1888.]—Examiners shall take an oath that they will faithfully discharge their

IV. TEACHERS —Continued.

duties; parish superintendent may in certain cases revoke the endorsements of teachers by examining committees.

77. [S. 47, A. 81, 1888.]—Qualifications necessary to obtain a third grade certificate.

78. [S. 48, A. 81, 1888.]—Qualifications for a second grade certificate.

79. [S. 49, A. 81, 1888.]—Qualifications for a third grade certificate.

80. [S. 50, A. 81, 1888.]—Certificate required as a requisite to the employment of a teacher.

81. [S. 3, A. 40, 1888]—Examination of teachers on hygiene and temperance.

82. [S. 4, A. 40, 1888.]—Certificate to be filed by teacher.

83. [S. 1, A. 57, 1894.]—Peabody Normal graduates are entitled to certificates of qualification.

84. [S. 51, A. 81, 1888.]—It is the duty of each teacher to keep daily registers, and to make monthly reports; penalty for non-performance.

85. [S. 52, A 81, 1888.]—Accountability of pupils to teachers.

INSTITUTES.

SEC. 55. [**Date for Teachers' Institute.**]—The parish superintendent may devote the first Saturday of each month, during the time the common schools are in session in the parish, to holding institutes for the improvement of teachers in their qualifications and methods of teaching, and for the discussion of topics pertaining to the advancement of the public school interest in the parish.

SEC. 56. [**Attendance Obligatory.**]—The teachers shall be notified of the time and place of the monthly institute meeting. Teachers failing to be present, or to take such part in the exercises as the Superintendent may assign or designate, shall forfeit one day's salary (which forfeited salary shall be paid to the parish institute fund), unless a good and sufficient reason for such failure to attend shall be given in writing to the parish superintendent within ten days thereafter. No teacher shall be bound to attend the institute who, to do so, shall have to travel a greater distance than ten miles each way, and otherwise than by land.

SEC. 57. [**Penalty for Superintendent's Absence.**]—Three hours work shall be required to constitute a legal session of one

institute, and the parish superintendent shall forfeit five dollars
for each institute that he fails to conduct as required by this
act, unless physically unable to attend, or for other sufficient
excuse, to the satisfaction of the school board.

SEC. 58. [Members May be Active or Honorary.]—These
institutes may receive as members, honorary or active, the members of the board, all officers, and any citizen of good moral
character as may desire to become a member, subject to the rules
and regulations, and to the payment of such dues and fines as
may be imposed by a quorum of the said institutes.

SEC. 59. [Parish Institutes; Roll of Members.]—Each parish superintendent, upon the assembling of the teachers' institute
of his parish shall cause a roll of the members to be prepared,
which roll shall be called at least twice a day during the session
of the institute, and all absentees shall be carefully marked.
He shall ascertain the number of teachers who were in attendance, and length of time each attended, and shall keep a record
thereof.

SEC. 60. [Institute Managers.]—Each parish superintendent before the beginning of the free school term, shall appoint
one of the best qualified teachers of his parish as institute manager for each institute district, should there be more than one
institute district in the parish ; and such appointees shall each
be paid for actual services two dollars and a half per day out of
the institute fund as compensation for holding institutes, and
for assisting the superintendent during the session.

SEC. 61. [Institute Fund.]—All institute funds shall be
collected and receipted for by the Superintendent. He shall
have a record of the amount received, hand them over to the
treasurer of the school board, who shall keep a separate account
of these funds. He shall pay them out on the warrant of the
superintendent, countersigned by the president of the school
board. These funds shall be expended only in the interest of
the institutes. The superintendent, for all services in connection
with these institutes, shall be paid three dollars a day out of

said fund for each day he will cause the said institute, to hold under his personal superintendence, and for each day's attendance as provided for in section fifty-five (55).

SEC. 62. [Institute Not Applicable to Orleans Parish]—The foregoing sections having reference to parish institutes shall not apply to the parish of Orleans, but the school board of said parish may inaugurate and carry on such institutes in the manner and with the power and authority set forth above.

SEC. 63. [Reports Respecting Institutes.]—The parish superintendent, in his annual report to the State Superintendent, shall state the time and place teachers' institutes were held; the names of the persons conducting the same; the number of persons registered as in attendance; the sums collected; the number and names of teachers of common schools in the parish who did not attend the institute, and such other information of the proceedings and results of the institute as he may deem of value and interest.

SEC. 64. [State Institutes.]—As a means of improving and making more efficient the teachers of the public schools of the State of Louisiana, and awakening a deeper public interest in said schools, the State Superintendent of Public Education and the President of the State Normal School shall cause to be held each year at least twenty (20) weeks of the State Teachers' Institutes at such times and places as they, with the advice of the respective parish superintendents of public education, may determine. They shall give notice of the time and place selected for each institute at least thirty days before the beginning of the said institute.

SEC. 65. [State Institute Conductor.]—The State Superin. tendent of Public Education and the President of the State Normal School shall select an experienced Institute Conductor, who shall have immediate charge of the institutes provided for in this act and whose salary for that service shall not exceed one thousand dollars ($1000) per annum, payable out of any funds donated by the board of trustees of the Peabody Educational Fund, or appropriated by the General Assembly of the State of Louisiana, for institute purposes.

SEC. 66. [**Ex-Officio Member of State Normal School Faculty.**] Said Institute Conductor shall be appointed for one year, and shall be ex-officio a member of the faculty of the State Normal School, performing therein such services and receiving such compensation therefor as the board of administrators of said institution may determine.

SEC. 67. [**Assistant's Remuneration.**]—Said Institute Conductor shall be assisted in the work by members of the faculty of the State Normal School and by such other assistants as the State Superintendent of Public Education and the President of the State Normal School may select; provided, that members of the State Normal School shall receive no compensation other than their actual traveling expenses for institute work done during the session of said institution; but for institute work done during the vacation of said Normal School. they, in common with the other assistants, shall receive such remuneration as the State Superintendent of Public Education and the President of the State Normal School may deem sufficient, payable out of any funds derived from the Peabody Fund, or appropriated by State, parish or locality for institute purposes.

SEC. 68. [**State Institute Managers.**]—The State Superintendent of Public Education, the President of the State Normal School and the State Institute Conductor shall be known as the State Institute Managers, and shall prescribe the order and character of the institute exercises and such other details as they may deem necessary.

SEC. 69. [**Notification to Teachers.**]—The parish superintendent, with the advice of the State Superintendent and the President of the State Normal School shall make all necessary arrangement for the State Teachers' Institutes held in his parish, and shall do everything in his power to insure their success. He shall give to every public school teacher of his parish at least fifteen days' notice of the time and place of meeting of the institute; and shall order all the public schools of his parish to be closed during the session of the institute.

SEC. 70. [Penalty for Absence Without Satisfactory Excuse.]— Any public school teacher failing to attend the institute held in his parish, without an excuse satisfactory to the board of school directors thereof, shall immediately upon demand of the parish superintendent, forfeit his certificate and lose his position; and each public school teacher in attendance upon the institute shall receive the same compensation for the time of attendance as for actual teaching, whether the school be in session or not; provided, he shall have been present during the whole session of the institute.

SEC. 71. [Leave of Absence and Compensation.]—The school superintendent of every parish in which no State institute is to be held during the year, shall encourage and urge the public school teachers of his parish to attend the nearest State Teachers Institute, granting them leave of absence from their school duties and giving them the same compensation for attending the institute as is provided in section seventy for the teachers of schools located in the parish wherein the institute is held.

SEC. 72. [Certificate of Attendance.]—The State Institute Conductor and his assistant conductors shall issue certificates of attendance to every teacher in attendance during the whole session of a State Teachers' Institute and parish boards of school directors shall give preference, *ceteris paribus*, to the holders of said certificates in the selection of teachers for the public schools.

SEC. 73. [Report of Institute Conductor.]—The State Institute Conductor shall annually make an exhaustive report of the State Teachers Institutes to the President of the State Normal School, who shall transmit said report to the State Superintendent of Public Education, and also embody it in his biennial report to the General Assembly.

EXAMINATIONS.

SEC. 74. [Competitive Examinations.]—It shall be the duty of the parish superintendent to conduct or superintend in person

3

the examination of all persons offering themselves as candidates for position of teachers of the common schools of his parish (except in cities and towns organized as one district by special act of the General Assembly; except also, when the applicant holds a certificate entitling him to teach without further examination, as provided for in this act), in regard to their moral character, learning and ability to teach. For any violation of this duty he shall be liable to a fine of not less than twenty dollars, nor more than fifty dollars. The school board of the parish shall appoint a committee of two competent persons to assist him (the parish superintendent) in making these examinations. The superintendent and the committee must agree as to competency of the applicant before a certificate can be issued. Whenever two or more teachers apply for the same position or positions a competitive examination shall be held, and the position or positions shall be given to the most competent.

SEC. 75. [**Examination Fee.**]—Before being examined, each applicant for a certificate to teach shall pay a fee of one dollar for the parish institute fund, which shall be returned to him if a certificate be not issued to him.

SEC. 76. [**Examiners; Duties and Penalties for Non-Performance.**]—Before the examiners shall commence their examination of teachers, they shall take an oath that they will faithfully discharge their duties; they shall not give to any person a certificate before they will have examined the candidate touching his or her qualifications and fitness to teach, and who is not qualified to teach as required by the common school law. They shall be satisfied that the applicant is possessed of good moral character; if at any time the teacher be found incompetent, inefficient or unworthy of the endorsement given him, the parish superintendent may revoke the same and notify the board of his action for its approval or disapproval. Any teacher may be discharged at any time under the above provisions, but he shall be entitled to receive payment for services only up to the time of such dismissal.

SEC. 77. [**Third Grade Certificate.**]—To obtain a third grade certificate the applicant must be found competent to teach spelling, reading, primary mental arithmetic, rudiments of practical arithmetic through fractions and simple interest, elementary geography, primary language lessons and laws of health.

SEC. 78. [**Second Grade Certificate.**]—To obtain a second grade certificate the applicant must be found competent to teach arithmetic, geography, English grammar and composition, United States history, elements of natural philosophy and elements of physiology.

SEC. 79. [**First Grade Certificate.**]—To obtain a high school or first grade certificate the applicant must be found competent to teach elocution, spelling, grammar, rhetoric and literature, history, botany, philosophy, arithmetic, algebra, geography and geometry, and such other studies of high grade as local boards may deem necessary. A special certificate of this grade may issue on a satisfactory examination in the study or studies to be taught in any special academic department, which shall entitle the holder to special appointment in a department where such studies may be taught.

SEC. 80. [**Certificate, a Requisite to Employment.**]—No person shall be appointed to teach who has not obtained a license for the scholastic year in which the school is to be taught, and of a grade sufficiently high to meet the requirements of the school, or unless he or she holds a certificate provided for by this act, which exempts him or her from examination; provided, that all teachers who have been teaching since three years are exempt from further examination.

SEC. 81. [**Additional Requirement.**]—No certificate shall be granted hereafter to any new applicant to teach in the public schools of Louisiana, who has not passed a satisfactory examination in the study of the nature of alcoholic drinks and narcotics, and of their effects upon the human system, in connection with the several divisions of the subject of relative physiology and hygiene.

SEC. 82. [Certificate to be Filed by the Teacher.]—Each teacher of any school in this State supported wholly or in part from public money, shall, before receiving any remuneration for services rendered in said capacity, file a certificate with the person by whom such payments are authorized to be made, to the effect that such teacher has faithfully complied with all the provisions of this act during the entire period for which such payment is sought and in the manner specified in this act, and no money shall be paid to any such teacher who has not filed such a certificate.

SEC. 83. [Exception in Regard to State and Peabody Normal Diplomas.]—Diplomas conferred by the Peabody Normal School, located at Nashville, Tennessee, upon graduates of that institution, shall entitle them to a first grade teacher's certificate, valid in any town or parish of this State for four years from the date of graduation, at the expiration of which time it may be renewed by the State Board of Education upon satisfactory evidence of the ability, progress, and moral character of the teacher making application for such renewal.

SEC. 84. Teacher's Register and Monthly Report.]—It shall be the duty of each teacher of a common school to keep such a register of the school as the parish superintendent may require, and prior to receiving his or her monthly salary at the end of each month, he or she shall make a report of the entire number of pupils enrolled; the highest, lowest and average number of pupils in attendance during the session; the books used, branches taught, number of pay pupils, if any, and such other information as the parish superintendent may deem important, and shall furnish a copy of such report to the parish superintendent, and if he or she willfully neglect or fail to do this the parish superintendent shall withhold two dollars ($2) of his salary due for the benefit of the parish institute.

SEC. 85. [Accountability of Pupils to Teachers.]—The teachers shall faithfully enforce in school the course of study and the regulations prescribed in pursuance of law, and if any teacher shall willfully refuse or neglect to comply with such requisitions, the parish superintendent, on petition or complaint which shall be deemed sufficient by the board, may remove or dismiss him or her. Eveiy teacher shall have the power and authority to hold every pupil to a strict accountability in school for any disorderly conduct on the play grounds of the school or during intermission or recess, and to suspend from school any pupil for good cause; provided, however, that such suspension shall be reported in writing as soon as practicable to the parish superintendent, whose decision of the case shall be final; and, provided further, that in the parish of Orleans the principals of schools shall suspend and report same to the superintendent for approval or further action.

V. REVENUE.

86. [S. 53, A. 81, 1888.]—Apportionment of current school fund by the State Superintendent.

87. [S. 54, A. 81, 1888.]—Police juries and municipal corporations, except New Orleans, to levy 1¼ mills for school purposes in their annual budget.

88. [S. 55, A. 81, 1888]—Fines and bonds forfeited to be collected for the support of the common schools.

89. [S. 1, A. 126, 1882.]—Special tax for public improvements; how levied.

90. [S. 3, A. 126, 1882.]—Advertisement of the result of election voting a special tax.

POLL TAX.

91. [S. 1, A. 120, 1880]—Poll tax; amount; upon whom levied.

92. [S. 2, A. 120, 1880.]—Poll tax operates as a lien or privilege.

93. [S. 4, A. 120, 1880.]—The collector of the poll tax to keep a record of taxes collected.

94. [S. 5, A. 120, 1880.]—Quarterly settlements to be made by the collector.

95. [S. 6, A. 120. 1880.]—How collector's quietus is obtained.

96. [S. 1, A. 89, 1888.]—Duty of assessor in listing poll tax payers, and penalty for non-performance.

97. [S. 2, A. 89, 1888.]—Sheriffs to return to the parish school boards a list of all persons who have paid poll taxes.

98. [S. 3, A. 89, 1888.]—Penalty for sheriff's failure to show cause for non-collection of tax.

99. [S. 4, A. 89, 1888.]—The sheriff may be compelled to show cause for not collecting.

100. [S. 1, A. 87, 1886.]—Poll tax receipt requisite to receiving witness or juror's compensation.

101. [S 2, A. 87, 1886.]—Deduction of witness and juror's compensation for poll tax.

102. [S. 3, A 87, 1886.]—Clerk of the

V. REVENUE—Continued.

court to notify the tax collector of such deductions.

103. [*S.* 1, *A.* 56, 1894.]—Collection of the poll tax of Orleans vested in the city treasurer.

SALE OF SCHOOL LANDS.

104. [*S.* 2958, *R. S.*, 1869.]—School lands: their sales; how to be made; duty of the parish treasurer.

105. [*S.* 2959, *R. S.*, 1869]—Survey of school lands.

106. [*S.* 2960, *R. S.*, 1869]—Sale on the order of the State Auditor.

107. [*S.* 1, *A.* 168, 1894.]—Sale of uninhabitable lands.

108. [*S.* 2, *A.* 168, 1894.]—Sale conducted like other sales.

109 [*S.* 2966, *R. S* , 1869.]—Sale of sections divided by parish lines

110. [*S.* 2660, *R. S.*, 1869]—Treasurer's commission in sales.

111. [*S.* 2962, *R. S.*, 1869.]—Lease of school lands.

112. [*S.* 2964, *R. S.*, 1869.]—Proceeds of lands accruing to townships.

113. [*S.* 2965, *R. S.*, 1869.]—Mode of annulling sales.

114. [*S.* 1, *A.* 57, 1884.—Duty of Auditor to provide for the collection of notes given in payment of the sixteenth sections

115. [*S.* 2, *A.* 57, 1884.] —Duty of parish treasurer in collecting said notes.

116. [*S.* 3, *A.* 57, 1884.] —Duty of district attorney or other attorney selected by school board to collect said notes; mode of proceeding in such collection.

117. [*S.* 4, *A.* 57, 1884.]—Attorney's compensation

118. [*Res.* 96, 1886.]—Duty of the Auditor in fixing the capital due the townships.

119. [*S.* 1, *A.* 14, 1882.]—Penalty for trespass on sixteenth section lands.

120. [*S.* 2, *A.* 14, 1882.]—Same.

DONATIONS.

121. [*S.* 1, *A.* 124, 1882.]—Donations, *inter viros* and *mortis causa*, authorized.

122. [*S.* 2, *A.* 124, 1882]—Conditions the donor may impose.

123. [*S.* 3, *A.* 124, 1882.]—Proviso, property cannot be made inalienable.

124. [*S.* 4, *A.* 124, 1882.]—Trustees to organize in a body corporate.

125. [*S.* 5, *A.* 124, 1882.] — When trustees fail to accept, the Governor may appoint others.

126. [*S.* 6, *A.* 124, 1882.]—Duty of the trustees.

127. [*S.* 7, *A.* 124, 1882.]—Duty of the trustees in accepting and administering other donations, *mortis causa* or *inter viros*.

128. [*S.* 8, *A.* 124, 1882.]—Substitutions *fidei commissæ* or trust disposition not to apply under this act.

129. [*S.* 6, *A.* 173, 1894.]—Disposition of funds of towns on the recision of their charters.

130. [*S.* 1, *A.* 103, 1880.]—Proscription of debts, etc.

SEC. 86. [**Apportionment of Current School Fund.**]—The State Superintendent of Public Education shall quarterly, on the first Monday in March, June, September and December, in each year, apportion the funds appropriated by the General Assembly for the support of the common schools of the State, among the several parishes of the State, according to the number of children between the ages of six and eighteen years in each parish; provided, however, that all the poll tax collected in any parish shall be appropriated to said parish. The amount so apportioned shall be paid by the State Treasurer to the school treasurer of each parish upon the warrant of the State Superintendent of Public Education.

SEC. 87. [**Police Jury and Municipal Tax.**]—The police jurors of the several parishes, and the boards of trustees, aldermen, and legal representatives of cities, towns and villages (except the parish of Orleans), may levy for the support of the common schools of their respective parishes, not less than one and a half mills of the ten mills tax on the dollar of the assessed valuation of the property thereof. This shall be provided for in their annual budgets. On the refusal or neglect to levy said tax or to vote for such levy, the parish school board shall have the right, and it shall be its duty, to compel by mandamus, which may be tried in chambers or in open court, the levy of said tax to be collected as in case of parish and corporation taxes, and shall be paid to the school treasury of the parish or town where collected, monthly, by the tax collector; provided, towns not exempted under their charters from the payment of parish taxes, and subjected to the burden of taxation as the parishes are, shall not pay this tax, for same is included in the taxes imposed by the parish in which the town is situated.

SEC. 88. [**Bonds and Fines.**]—All fines imposed by the several district courts for violation of law and the amount collected on all forfeited bonds in criminal cases, after deducting commissions, shall be paid over by the sheriff of the parish in which the same are imposed and collected, to the treasurers of the school boards in said parishes, and shall be applied to the support of the common schools, as are applied to other funds levied for the purpose (the parish of Orleans excepted.)

SEC. 89.* [Special Tax; How Levied.]—Whenever one-tenth of the property tax payers of any parish, city, incorporated town or municipality in this State shall petition the police jury, city, town or municipal authorities to levy an increased rate of taxation for the purpose of constructing public buildings, bridges without draws and works of public improvements in such parish, city, town or municipality, the said police jury, city, town or municipal authorities shall order a special election for that purpose, and shall submit to a vote of the property tax payers of such parish, city, town or municipality entitled to vote under the election laws of the State, the rate of taxation and the purpose for which it is intended: *provided*, that said election be held under the general election laws of the State at that time in force, and at the polling places at which the last preceding general election was held, and not sooner than twenty days after the official publication of the petition and ordinance ordering the election, which shall be made in the same manner provided by law for judicial advertisement.

SEC. 90. [Publication.]—The publication of the result of said election shall be made by ten days advertisement immediately thereafter, and the police juries, city, town and municipal authorities shall have the same power to enforce the collection of any special tax that may be authorized by said election as by law provided for the collection of other taxes.

POLL TAX.

SEC. 91. [Poll Tax; Amount; Upon Whom Levied.]—In pursuance to the requirements and authorization of Art. 208 of the Constitution of the State, a poll tax of one dollar *per capita* shall be and is hereby levied, annually, upon each male inhabitant of the State over the age of twenty-one years, said tax to be due and payable on and after the first day in January in each year.

---

*SECTION 89. The law authorizes the levy of a special tax for the erection of public buildings and other improvements.

A school house is a public building for the free public schools, and it certainly is a public improvement.

Sec. 92. [**Operates as a Lien and Privilege.**]—The said poll tax shall operate as a first privilege and lien on all real and personal property, of whatever kind, which may be owned by, or to which the said tax payer may have any right, for the year he may owe the tax, and such privilege shall continue to exist thereon into whatever hands such property or right may pass and shall not be prescribed, and the collector of such tax shall have the right at any time after such tax shall be payable, and after the first day of January in each year, to seize any such property or rights, and to cause the same to be sold, after ten days' notice given, the same as in notices of sale under execution, to pay the said tax and the costs of seizure and sale, which costs shall not exceed five dollars in each case.

Sec. 93. [**Book to be Kept by the Collector.**]—The collector of the poll tax shall keep a book in which he shall enter the tax as paid. He shall, in said book, give the name of the party paying or for whom the tax is paid, the date of the payment, and by whom paid, and the amount paid, which entry shall be made when the payment is made, or within three days after the payment, and all payments so made shall be entered in such book made previous to any day of settlement; and at each settlement the collector shall make affidavits to the above requirements.

Sec. 94. [**Quarterly Settlements by the Collector.**]—The collector of said poll tax shall make settlements for every three months, counting from the first day of January in each year, with the authority, authorized by law, to settle with him therefor in each parish.

Sec. 95.* [**How Collector's Quietus is to be Obtained.**]—The collector of the poll tax, or his securities, shall not be released from their responsibility for the collection of such tax or have a *quietus* therefor until he shall satisfy the parish school board, or other school authority of the parish, created under and according

* "To obtain his discharge, an officer should obtain a clear receipt from the board of school directors, in so far as he has incurred any responsibility as an officer in which the said board is concerned.—33d *Ann.* 709; *State ex rel. vs. Sheriff.*

to Article 225 of the Constitution, that the same cannot be collected, and such collector shall account for all moneys collected by him as poll tax for the year. A final settlement of such poll tax shall be made by the collector each year, on or before the thirty-first day of December.

SEC. 96. [Collection of the Poll Tax.]—The assessors are hereby required to render to the school boards of their respective parishes, annually, by the first Saturday of October, a complete schedule list, by wards, of all persons liable to pay a poll tax in their respective parishes. If any assessor fails to comply with the requirement of this act, the failure shall be cause for removal; besides, he shall be subject to a fine of $250, for the benefit of the public schools in the parish in which the delinquent officer resides, and in which he is the assessor. In the city of New Orleans the board of assessors shall comply with the requirement of this act, and in the event of failure, shall be subject to dismissal and penalty as before provided.

SEC. 97. [Returns of Collections.]—The sheriffs and tax collectors in their respective parishes shall return, by the first Saturday of February, of each and every year, to the school boards of their respective parishes, a list predicated upon the list before mentioned by wards, showing all persons in the parishes respectively, who have paid their poll tax, as well as persons who have not paid the same, and shall return their reasons in writing and under oath, the cause in each instance of the non-payment of a poll tax, and why they have not collected the tax not collected.

SEC. 98. [Penalties.]—If the said sheriff or tax collector fails to show cause why the said poll tax has not been collected, he shall be responsible for and shall pay the poll taxes he has failed to collect, and shall be held liable with his securities on his official bond for the payment of said tax.

SEC. 99. [Rule for Non-Compliance.]—The sheriff can be made to show cause why the said poll tax has not been collected, at chambers, before the district judge, after service of rule and three days have elapsed after service.

SEC. 100. [Receipt for the Poll Tax.]—Before persons serving as jurors or as witnesses in criminal cases shall receive the compensation to which they are entitled for their mileage and *per diem*, they shall exhibit to the clerk of the court a receipt for the poll tax or taxes due by them.

SEC. 101. **[Deduction of Witnesses' and Jurors' Compensation, for Poll Tax.]**—On their failure to produce such receipt the clerk of the court, or other officer, issuing certificates or warrants for their *mileage* and *per diem*, shall issue certificates or warrants for amount less the poll tax due, and shall issue the certificate or warrants for amount so reserved for poll tax, to the treasurer of the school board of the parish, who shall collect same.

SEC. 102. **[Report by the Clerk of Court.]**—The clerk of court or other officer, issuing such certificates or warrants, shall report to the tax collector of the parish the names of all persons from whom he has reserved amounts for poll tax, and the tax collector shall give such person credit for such poll tax.

SEC. 103. **[Poll Tax Collections of Orleans.]**—The collection of poll taxes in the parish of Orleans, together with all the processes, commissions and obligations incident thereto as now provided by law, are vested in the treasurer of the city of New Orleans.

SALE OF SCHOOL LANDS.

SEC. 104. **[Election.]**—It shall be the duty of the parish treasurers of the several parishes in this State to have taken the sense of the inhabitants of the township, to which they may belong, any lands heretofore reserved and appropriated by Congress for the use of schools, whether or not the same shall be sold, and the proceeds invested as authorized by an act of Congress approved February 15, 1843. Polls shall be opened and held in each township, after advertisement, for thirty days at three of the most public places in the town, and at the courthouse door, and the sense of the legal voters therein shall be taken within the usual hours, and in the usual manner of holding elections, which elections shall be held and votes received by a member of the parish school board or a justice of the peace ; and if a majority of the legal voters be in favor of selling the school lands therein, the same may be sold, but not otherwise. The result of all such elections shall be transmitted to the parish treasurer, and by him to the State Superintendent.

SEC. 105. [**Survey.**]—Before making sale of the school lands belonging to the State, it shall be the duty of the parish treasurer, or other persons whose duty it may become to superintend the sales, to cause a re-survey of such lines as from any cause may have become obliterated or uncertain ; and for this purpose he is authorized to employ the parish surveyor, or on his default, any competent surveyor ; and the lines thus surveyed shall be marked in such manner as to enable those interested to make a thorough examination before sale, and all advertisements made for the sale of such lands shall contain a full description thereof according to the original survey and that required by this section. The expenses of the survey shall be paid by the Auditor of Public Accounts out of the proceeds of the sale of the lands on the warrants of the parish treasurer.

SEC. 106. [**Sale on the Order of the Auditor.**]—If the majority of the votes taken in a township shall give their assent to the sale of the lands aforesaid, the parish treasurer shall forthwith notify the Auditor of Public Accounts of the vote thus taken, and upon his order, the said lands shall be sold by the parish treasurer, at public auction, before the courthouse door, by the sheriff or an auctioneer to be employed by the treasurer at his expense, to the highest bidder, in quantities not less than 40 acres, nor more than 160, after having been previously appraised by three sworn appraisers, selected by the parish treasurer and recorder of the parish, after thirty (30) days' advertisement, but in no case at a less sum than the appraised value, payable on a credit of ten years, as follows : ten per cent in cash and the balance in nine annual installments, the interest to be paid on the whole amount, annually, at the rate of eight per cent *per annum;* the notes shall be made payable to the Auditor of Public Accounts, secured by special mortgage on the land sold, and personal security *in solido*, until final payment of principal and interest; in the event of the purchaser neglecting or refusing to pay any of these installments or interest at maturity, the mortgage shall be forthwith closed, and the parish treasurer is hereby authorized to advertise and sell the land as before provided for, and further authorized and required to execute all acts of sale on behalf of the State for any such lands sold, to receive the cash payment and notes given for the purchase, which shall be made payable to the State Treasurer, and to place the same in the office of the Auditor of Public Accounts, for collection; all cash received, either for principal or interest, from said sales shall be transmitted by him to the State Treasurer, and any moneys thus received into the State treasury from sales aforesaid shall bear interest at the rate of six per cent *per annum*, and be credited to the township to which the same belongs according to the provisions of the act of Congress. The parish treasurer shall forthwith notify the State Superintendent of the result of all sales made by him. The parish treasurer shall be authorized to receive the whole amount bid for the lands, deducting the eight per cent interest which the credits will bear.

SEC. 107. [**Sale of Unhabitable Lands.**]—All sixteenth section lands located in a township not habitable by reason of the land being swamp or sea marsh, the school board of the parish in which such lands are located may present an application for sale of such sixteenth section land to the Auditor of Public Accounts, in which they shall set forth the location of the township, its character and the reason upon which a sale is desired and upon receipt of such application duly signed by the president and secretary thereof, the Auditor may authorize the sale, if in his judgment a sale should be made.

SEC. 108. [**Sale Conducted in the Same Manner as Others.**]— In case a sale is ordered as provided for in section one of this act, the parish treasurer shall make such sale in the same manner, and upon the terms and conditions as is now provided by law for the sale of sixteenth section lands; provided this act shall not apply to sixteenth sections now leased to parties for a term of years.

SEC. 109. [**Sale of Sections Divided by Parish Lines.**]—When the sixteenth section of any township is divided by a parish line, the treasurer of the parish in which a greater portion of the section may lie, shall proceed to take the sense of the people of the township, and to sell the same as provided by law, as if the whole section lay in his parish; provided, that the same shall be advertised at the courthouse of both parishes.

SEC. 110. [**Treasurer's Commission.**]—Parish treasurers of the several parishes shall be entitled to retain out of the proceeds of the sale of sixteenth sections effected by them a percentage of 2½ on the amount of said sales, to be deducted from the cash payment, and the same shall be in full compensation of their services.

SEC. 111. [**Lease of School Lands.**]—Should a majority of the legal votes be against the sale of the lands, then it shall be the duty of the parish board of directors, where the same may be situated, to secure them from injury and waste, and prevent illegal possession or aggression of any kind, and in conjunction with the parish treasurer to lease the same, or any part thereof, for a term not exceeding four years, according to the provisions of the second section of the act of Congress aforesaid, and to inform the Superintendent thereof.

SEC. 112. [**Proceeds of Lands Accruing to Townships.**]—All moneys that have been or may be hereafter received into the State treasury, and the interest that has or may accrue thereon from the sale of any sixteenth section of school lands or the school land warrants belonging to the various townships in the State, shall be placed to the credit of the township, and should the people of any township desire to receive for the use of the schools therein, the annual interest payable by the State on funds deposited to their credit, or the annual proceeds of the loan, the parish treasurer shall, on the petition of five legal voters in any such township, order an election to be held in the township, as provided for the sale of township lands; and if a majority of any number of votes above seven be in favor of receiving annually the accruing interest as aforesaid, the same shall be paid to the treasurer of the parish for the use of the townships or districts; otherwise the interest shall be an accumulated fund to their credit until so called for.

SEC. 113. [**Mode of Annulling Sales.**]—In all cases of the sale of the school lands known as sixteenth sections, heretofore made, where the purchase money has not been paid, the purchaser or purchasers shall have the right to annul the sale upon application to the district court of the parish where the land is situated; provided, that the judgment of nullity shall be obtained at the cost of the applicant and contradictorily with the district attorney, in conjunction with the school directors of the district in which said land is situated, who shall be made a party defendant in such suit; provided, also, that it shall appear upon the hearing that the value of the land has not been impaired by any act of the purchaser; and provided further, that nothing in this act shall be so construed as to entitle the said purchaser to repayment of any part of the purchase money already paid.

SEC. 114. [**Auditor's Duty in the Collection of Notes.**]—It shall be the duty of the Auditor of Public Accounts, immediately on the passage of this act, to forward for collection to the treasurer of the school board in their respective parishes throughout the State, all the notes given for the purchase price of sixteenth sections, or any part thereof, known as free school lands, whenever any installment of said purchase price has become due or may become due, and it shall be the duty of said treasurer of parish school board to receive and receipt for same.

SEC. 115. [**Parish Treasurer's Duty in the Collection of Notes.**] It shall be the duty of the treasurer of the parish school

board, on receipt of the notes due and given for the said sixteenth sections, to immediately notify the principal and his
sureties, in writing, of the amount of said note, principal and
interest, due and unpaid; provided, said lands for which said
notes were given are still in possession of the original purchaser,
and it in the possession of other parties, such possessor shall
also be likewise notified of all the demands, principal and
interest, against said lands, and if all the demands against the
same be not satisfied within thirty days from said notice, it shall
be the duty of the treasurer of the parish school board to turn
over said notes to the district attorney for said district, or other
attorney selected by the school board, for suit; and, provided
further, that said notice shall serve as a bar to prescription,
which shall only begin to run from the service of said notice.

SEC. 116. [**Attorney's Duty in the Collection of Notes.**]—It
shall be the duty of the said attorney to proceed without delay,
by all necessary legal processes, and without depositing clerk's
or sheriff's costs, or giving security therefor, to collect all such
notes as may be turned over to him by said treasurer of the
parish school board, and given for sixteenth sections, known as
free school lands, and if any of the conservatory writs should be
found to be necessary in order to aid in said collection, it shall
be lawful to issue the same, without giving bond as required in
other cases.

SEC. 117. [**Attorney's Compensation.**]—The said attorney shall
receive ten per cent of all money collected by him on notes
given for sixteenth sections, and after deducting said ten per
cent he shall turn over the remainder to the treasurer of the
school funds for the parish in which said lands are situated,
and the same shall be transmitted through the Auditor of
Accounts, by said treasurer, to the State Treasurer; and any
moneys thus received into the State Treasury from said collections shall bear interest at the rate of four per cent per annum,
and be credited to the township to which the same belongs,
according to the provisions of the Act of Congress.

Sec. 118. [Duty of the Auditor in Fixing Capital Due the Townships.]—It shall be the duty of the Auditor of Public Accounts, by the 1st day of January, 1887, to ascertain the amount of capital that may be due the several townships from the proceeds of the sales of sixteenth sections, made since the 1st of January, 1880, and actually paid into the State Treasury. The amount thus ascertained shall be the capital upon which interest shall be thereafter allowed and paid out of the interest collected on the said bonds to the townships, the sixteenth sections of which have been sold since the 1st of January, 1880, and the proceeds actually paid into the State Treasury, and the proceeds so paid invested as required by law.

In calculating the interest due the several townships, no interest shall be allowed for fractions of the year during which the receipts shall have come into the treasury; but it shall commence at the beginning or the 1st of January of the next year.

The interest due upon the capital ascertained as aforesaid, and the interest due upon subsequent sales, shall be paid to the townships in the manner now provided for by law. It shall be the duty of the Auditor to furnish the Treasurer and Superintendent of Public Education with a statement of the amount due each township.

Sec. 119. [Trespass on Sixteenth Sections.]—Whoever shal cut down, or remove for sale for his own use, or the use of another, any timber on any free school land in this State, belonging to the State, known as sixteenth sections, shall be deemed guilty of a misdemeanor, and upon conviction shall be condemned to pay a fine of not less than fifty nor more than one thousand dollars, and in default of the same, be sentenced to imprisonment not less than ten days nor more than one year.

Sec. 120. [Same.]—Whoever shall knowingly use, cultivate or inclose any free school land, known as the sixteenth section, without authority from the parish board of school directors, shall on conviction be condemned to pay a fine of not less than fifty nor more than one thousand dollars, and in default of the same

4

be sentenced to imprisonment for not less than ten days nor more than one year.

DONATIONS.

SEC. 121. [Donations Authorized.]—Any one can make a donation of any description of property and to any amount to trustees for educational, charitable or literary purposes, or for the benefit of educational, charitable or literary institutions whether already existing, or thereafter to be founded.

SEC. 122. [Conditions the Donor May Impose.]—The donor shall have the right to prescribe the number of trustees; the causes for which the trustees shall cease to be such; the manner in which vacancies shall be filled and the manner and formalities the trustees shall follow in transacting business.

SEC. 123. [Property Cannot be Made Inalienable.]—The donor shall have the right to prescribe the manner in which the property donated shall be administered, and the objects to which it or any part thereof, or the revenues thereof, shall be applied; provided, however, that property donated cannot be made inalienable; but the donor thereof shall have the right to prescribe in what manner and under what circumstances the trustees shall be empowered to sell the same, or any portion thereof, or to change any investment once made.

SEC. 124. [Trustees to Organize in a Body Corporate.]—The trustees named in the act of donation and their successors or substitutes, or such of them as are willing and may accept the trust, shall, upon complying with the laws of this State, relative to the organization of corporations for literary, scientific, religious and charitable purposes, constitute a body corporate with the power of continuous succession and unlimited duration, and with all the powers conferred upon corporations by said law or by custom; provided, however, that the requirem nt of said law, as to the number of persons necessary for the formation of a corporation, shall not apply to such trustees; and, provided further, that if any of the trustees will not or cannot accept the trust, then such of those named as are willing, may accept, and, in the manner prescribed in the act of donation, proceed to fill the vacancies up to the required number.

SEC. 125. [**When Trustees Fail to Accept, the Governor May Appoint Others.**]—Whenever there is an entire failure of the trustees to accept, the Governor of the State may name a number of persons equal to the number named by the donor, and who shall fill the places of, and be vested with all the powers conferred upon the trustees by said donor.

SEC. 126. [**Duty of the Trustees.**]—The board of trustees shall administer the property entrusted to them in conformity with the directions contained in the act of donation, and shall have all the powers needed in such administration; but cannot mortgage nor encumber the donated property, except as may be prescribed in the act of donation. And said trustees shall not be entitled to any remuneration for their services, unless expressly granted in the act of donation.

SEC. 127. [**Duty of Trustees Respecting Other Donations.**]—Said board of trustees shall have the power to accept and administer other donations *mortis causa* or *inter vivos* from the same or other, and to apply the same as may be prescribed in the subsequent act of donations. The administration of such subsequent act of donations, to be governed by the directions contained in the subsequent act of donation.

SEC. 128. [**Fidei Commissæ.**]—The provisions contained in the Revised Civil Code, or other laws of the State relative to substitious *fidei commissæ* or trust dispositions, shall not be deemed to apply to, or in any manner affect donations made for the purposes and in the manner provided by this act, and all laws or parts of laws conflicting with the provisions of this act, are repealed in so far as regards the purposes of this act, but not otherwise.

SEC. 129. [**Disposition of Funds of Towns on the Recission of Their Charters.**]—If after paying all the debts of said town (upon the dissolution and recission of its charter) there shall remain any balance of money, the same shall be turned over to the School Board of the parish to be used in the education of the children of school age residing within the territory covered by said town.

SEC. 130 [**Prescription of Debts, Etc.**]—The term of prescription of any and all debts, due to any charitable institution in this State, and to any college fund, or any fund of any institution of learning, or to any fund bequeathed for charitable purposes, for the purpose of distribution to the poor or indigent, or for purposes of education, and of all debts contracted by borrowing the whole or part of any such funds, shall be thirty years; provided, the debt is evidenced by writing.

VI. SCHOOLS.

131. [*S.* 10, *A.* 81, 1888.]—Graded and high schools: authorization to be given by the State Board of Education; assessment of one dollar to provide the common schools with fuel

132. [*S.* 14, *A.* 81, 1888.]—Branches to be taught.

133. [*S.* 1, *A.* 40, 1888.]—Instruction in hygiene and temperance.

134. [*S.* 2, *A.* 40, 1888.]—Text-books shall give due attention to the subject of alcoholic drinks and

their effects upon the human system.

135. [*S.* 1 *A.* 52, 1894.]—Combination with sectarian schools prohibited.

136. [*S.* 2, *A.* 52, 1894.]—Penalty for violation of the above regulation.

137. [*S.* 1, *A.* 93, 1892.]—Legal holidays.

138. [*S.* 1304. *R. S.*, 1869.]—Free passage over streams for children.

139. [*S.* 6, *A.* 70, 1882.]—Limit of school attendance.

SEC. 131. [**Graded and High Schools.**]—The parish school board shall have the authority to establish graded schools, and to adopt such a system in that connection as may be necessary to assure their success; central or high schools may be established when necessary.* The ordinances establishing such schools adopted by the parish school boards shall be submitted to the State Board of Education, and no high school shall be opened without its sanction, and no such school shall be established

*SECTION 131. "*Be it Resolved*, That the State Board of Education calls the attention of the parish boards to the necessity of establishing high schools wherever the high grade of students justifies it, as the State Board of Education believe that the establishment of a number of high schools in the State will contribute powerfully to build up both the public school system and colleges and universities."—*Proceedings, State Board of Education, August* 18, 1892.

unless the amount be donated for the site and suitable buildings are provided for without any expense out of the school fund; provided, that the boards of directors of the parish of Orleans shall not require the sanction of the State Board for the purposes aforesaid. The school boards shall have the authority to assess and collect one dollar per annum from each family, surviving parent or guardian, who actually sends a child or children to the common schools of the district, to be collected in such manner as said board shall determine, which amount shall be used in providing the school house with fuel and defraying the expenses necessary for the comfort of the school.

SEC. 132. [**Branches to be Taught.**]—The branches of orthography, reading, writing, arithmetic, geography, grammar, United States history and laws of health and physical education shall be taught in every district. In addition to those, such other branches as the State Board of Education and the parish school board may require; provided, that these elementary branches may be also taught in the French language in those parishes in the State or localities in said parishes where the French language predominates, if no additional expense is incurred.

SEC. 133. [**Hygiene and Temperance.**]—In addition to the branches, in which instrution is now given in the public schools, instruction shall also be given as to the nature of alcoholic drinks and narcotics, and special instruction as to their effects upon the human system in connection with the several divisions of the subject of relative physiology and hygiene, and such subjects shall be taught as regularly as other branches are taught in said schools. Such instruction shall be given orally from a text book in the hand of the teacher, to pupils who are not able to read, and shall be given by the use of text books in the hands of the pupils in the case of those who are able to read, and such instruction shall be given as aforesaid to all pupils in all public schools in the State, to all the grades until completed in the high schools.

SEC. 134. [Text Books.]—The text books used for the instruction required to be given by the preceding section *(referring to the law in regard to the teaching of Hygiene and Temperance,)* shall give at least one-fourth of their space to the consideration of the nature and effects of alcoholic drinks and narcotics; and the books used in the highest grades of graded schools shall contain at least twenty pages of matter relating to this subject.

Text books on physiology in use in the schools or at the time this act takes effect, which are not in accordance with the requirements of this section, except when previous contracts as to such text books now in force.

SEC. 135. [Sectarian Schools.]—The Boards of School Directors of the several parishes of this State are prohibited from entering into any contract, agreement, understanding, or combination, tacitly or expressly, directly or indirectly with any church, monastic or other religious order or association of any religious sect or denomination whatsoever, or with the representatives thereof, for the purpose of running or to defray the expenses for the running of any public school or schools of this State, together in connection or in combination with any private or parochial school or other institution of learning which may be under the control, authority, supervision, administration or management of any church, monastic, or other religious order or association of any religious sect or denomination whatsoever.

SEC. 136. [Penalty.]—The violation of the provisions of this act by the Board of School Directors or any member thereof shall be cause for their removal.

SEC. 137. [Days of Rest.]—The following shall be considered as days of public rest and legal holidays and half holidays in this State, and no others, namely: Sundays, the first of January, the eighth of January, the twenty-second of February, Good Friday, the fourth of July, the first of November, the twenty-fifth of December, Thanksgiving Day as designated by the President of the United States, and, in the parish of Orleans, Mardi-Gras and the twenty-fifth of November, to be known as "Labor Day."

SEC. 138. [**Free Passage Over Streams for Pupils.**]—The free right of passage or conveyance, over all public ferries, bridges and roads (except the ferries of the Mississippi River) which are rented out by the State or parish, or over which the State or parish exercises any control, or for which license is paid or toll exacted, be and is hereby granted to all children on foot attending free public schools, and no tolls or fees shall be demanded or exacted from said children by the keepers or attendants of said ferries, bridges or roads in their passage to and from schools between the hours of 7 o'clock A. M. and 9 o'clock A. M., and *four* o'clock P. M. and *six* o'clock P. M.; provided, that on Sundays and holidays no scholar shall have the right to cross such ferries, bridges or roads on terms different from those of any ordinary passenger.

SEC. 139. [**Limit of Attendance in Charge of One Teacher.**]—No school of less than ten pupils shall be opened or maintained in any locality; nor shall more than forty pupils be placed in charge of any one teacher.

VII. CITY SCHOOLS.

140. [*S.* 62, *A.* 81, 1888.]—Board of directors; how appointed; how vacancies are filled.

141. [*S.* 1, *A.* 158, 1894, *amending and re-enacting Section* 63 *of Act* 81 *of* 1888.]—Board of school directors: a body corporate; quorum; legal process served on the president or vice-president; attorney; organization. Secretary: must not be a member of the board; duties and salary.

142. [*S.* 64, *A.* 81, 1888.]—Additional powers of the board of directors; the adjustment of the salaries of teachers, porters and portresses; limitation of annual and monthly expenditures; rules for competitive examinations; election of teachers from among candidates holding certificates, and graduates of normal schools; regular monthly meetings; vacating seats of members of board for absence from two successive meetings and other causes; evening and night schools; normal schools.

143. [*S.* 65, *A.* 81, 1888.]—No compensation allowed to directors.

144. [*S.* 2, *A.* 158, 1894.]—Superintendent: his duties, powers, salary, and term of office.

145. [*S.* 1, *A.* 136, 1894.]—School taxes collected prior to 1880 to be turned over to the Board of Liquidation.

146. [*S* 2, *A.* 136, 1894.]—Duty of the board in certain cases.

VII. CITY SCHOOLS—Continued.

147. [S. 3, A. 136, 1894.]—Duty of the Board of Liquidation.

148. [S. 67, A. 81, 1888.]—City treasurer; ex-officio school treasurer; bond.

149. [S. 68, A. 81, 1888.]—Treasurer's term of office; removal; election of a successor.

150. [S. 69, A. 81, 1888.—Mayor, treasurer, and comptroller of the city of New Orleans, ex-officio members of the board; cannot vote.

151. [S. 70, A. 81, 1888.]—Report of the board.

152. [S. 71, A. 81, 1888.]—Budget of expenses: what it shall include.

153. [S. 72, A. 81. 1888.]—Provisions for affording proper evidence of claim.

SEC. 140. [Orleans School Board.]—All the public schools of the parish of Orleans, and the property and appurtenances thereof, shall be under the direction and control of a board of directors. Said board shall consist of twenty members, eight of whom shall be appointed by the Governor, by and with the consent and approval of the State board of education, and twelve members thereof shall be elected by the city council of New Orleans. The members of said board shall hold office during four years after their appointment and election, except as hereinafter provided, and until their successors are appointed or elected and qualified. On the first organization of said board by the members thereof, who shall be appointed and elected on the passage hereof, and in the manner aforesaid, the members shall be divided into four classes, by such method as they may choose, each class to consist of three members, elected by the city council and two members appointed by the Governor, by and with the consent and approval of the State board of education, whose terms shall expire respectively in one, two, three and four years, and whose successors shall be elected and appointed for four years, and in the manner set forth above; so that one-fourth of the membership of said board shall expire, and be elected and appointed annually. Vacancies in membership shall be filled by the appointive or elective power, as herein provided.

SEC. 141. [Powers and Duties of the Board.]—Said board of directors of the public schools of the parish of Orleans, shall be a body corporate in law, with power to sue and be sued. Eleven members shall constitute a quorum for the transaction of business. Legal process shall be served on the president; in his absence or inability to act, on the vice president. The city attorney shall act as attorney for the board. The board shall be organized within ten days after its appointment, with a president and vice president chosen from among its members, and a secretary, who shall not be a member of the board. In addition to the duties of his office, which may be fully prescribed by the board, he shall make a quarterly report to the State Superintendent of Education of the cost of maintaining the city schools, and shall keep the accounts of said board in such manner as to be in strict accordance with such budget as they may adopt, certifying to said board at each monthly meeting the expenses of said board for each current month. Said board shall have control of all buildings, records, papers, furniture and property of any kind pertaining to the administration of the schools, and shall have management of all the public schools within the limits of the city of New Orleans.

The salary of the secretary which shall be fixed by the board, shall be paid in the same manner as hereinafter provided for the payment of the superintendent.

SEC. 142. [**Authority of the Directors; Duties.**]—In addition to the powers and duties hereinbefore granted to and imposed upon parish boards, the powers and duties of said board of directors of the parish of Orleans shall be as follows:

First—It shall adjust and fix equitably the salaries of teachers and porters or portresses employed in the schools, and of the secretary and employees and of such assistant superintendents as it may deem necessary for an efficient supervision of the schools.

Second—It shall limit the annual expenses of maintaining the schools to the annual revenue, and the expense for any one month shall not exceed the one ninth part of the whole amount provided for the schools.

Third—It shall prescribe rules for subjecting teachers, or candidates for teacherships, to a careful competitive examination on all such branches as they are expected to teach, and no person shall be elected to a position as teacher without a favorable report on his or her moral and mental qualificfitions by an organized committee of examiners appointed by the board. Teachers regularly examined and elected shall not be removed from the schools during the time for which employed, except on written charges of immorality, neglect of duty, incompetency or malfeasance, of which he or she have been found guilty by a majority of the members of the board at a regular monthly meeting. The said board may except from such examination any person who has passed a satisfactory examination, as required by Act No. 23 of 1877, approved March twenty-sixth (26th), eighteen hundred and seventy-seven (1877), and who holds a certificate of qualification, and who has had two years or more experience as a teacher, so that the calling of a teacher shall be elevated to a profession, and that a system of life certificates shall be issued to all such teachers in the city of New Orleans by the board of directors of city schools; any person who is a graduate of a State normal school, or of any college or university duly authorized to confer degrees, certificates of qualifications shall be given to all persons who successfully pass such examination.

Fourth—It shall elect all teachers from among the candidates holding certificates in the order of their merit, as shown by such examination, including graduates of normal schools, as shown by the averages attained at their final examinations, or from among persons excepted from examinations as hereinbefore provided.

Fifth—All certificates to teachers granted hereafter shall stand good for three years; upon a second examination at the end of three years, certificates of a higher grade shall be given, to be good for five years, if the applicant is found competent to teach a higher grade school than the one for which the first certificate issued.

Sixth—It shall hold regular monthly meetings on a day fixed by it.

Seventh—It shall declare vacant the position of any of its members who shall have failed to perform the duties assigned to him, or have absented himself from two successive monthly meetings of the board without leave, or have been guilty of any breach of decorum, or of any other act inconsistent with the dignity of a school director; and it shall report each vacancy to the body by which the delinquent member shall have been previously elected or appointed; it shall be the duty of the board of directors of city schools elected and appointed under the provisions of this act to examine and scrutinize personally the accounts of their predecessors, in order to find out if their administration of the school funds, committed to their charge for . disbursement, has been in accordance with law, so that in the future a proper administration of the city schools may be had.

Eighth—It may establish, when practicable, evening or night schools for the instruction of such youths as are prevented by their daily vocations from receiving instructions during the day.

Ninth—It may establish, when deemed advisable, one or more normal schools or departments for the professional training and improvement of candidates for teacherships, including, in the course of instruction and training, lectures in the natural sciences, and on the method of teaching and disciplining children, and the practical exercises of non-teaching students in model classes organized for that purpose by the faculty of the institution. To graduates of these normal schools or departments, and also to proficient students in other city schools of an academic grade, the board may, in its discretion, award diplomas; and the graduates of the normal schools or departments who shall have been examined and found proficient in all the branches required to be taught in the public grammar schools, may be deemed preferred candidates for vacant positions in the city public schools, and the diplomas awarded to such graduates shall be deemed equivalent to teaching certificates of the highest grade for common schools; provided, that the final examinations for graduation from said normal schools, and upon which diplomas may be awarded, shall be conducted in the same manner and include the same subjects as the public competitive examinations required by paragraph three (3) of this section.

SEC. 143.   [Services of the Directors Without Compensation.]—No school director of the city of New Orleans shall receive compensation for his services as a school director.

SEC. 144.   [Superintendent—Duties, Authority, Salary.]—The said board is authorized to appoint for the constant supervision and periodical examination of the public schools of the parish of Orleans, a competent and experienced educator to be designated as superintendent. He shall aid the directors in organizing the schools and in improving the methods of instruction therein, in examining candidates for teacherships, and in conducting periodical examinations of pupils for promotion through the respective grades of the schools, and in maintaining general uniformity and discipline in the management of all the schools. He shall make semi-annual reports on the condition and needs of the schools to the said board, and an annual report on or before the first of January to the State board of education, as hereinbefore required; and, whenever notified to be present. he shall attend meetings of the State board of education.

The superintendent shall receive an annual salary of twenty-five hundred dollars, payable in equal monthly installments, payable on the roll of the board of directors of the city schools, in the same manner and at the same time that the employees and expenses of said board of directors are pa d. He shall hold his office for the term of four years, subject to removal by the board for neglect of duty or malfeasance, of which, after an impartial hearing by the board, he shall have been adjudged guilty. He shall be ex-officio a member of said board, and entitled to participate in its deliberations and debates, and in the examination of candidates for teacherships, but he shall not cast a vote in the board.

SEC. 145. [**Taxes Prior to 1880.**]—All the school taxes collected by the city of New Orleans prior to 1880 be turned over to the Board of Liquidation of the city debt of New Orleans.

SEC. 146. [**Judgment Against the School Board.**]—Whenever a judgment shall be rendered or has heretofore been rendered against the board of School Directors of the city of New Orleans, whether the same be absolute against the School Board, or payable out of the school taxes levied by the city of New Orleans for any particular year or years, and the same shall have become final and executory, the plaintiff in the suit shall cause a copy of the petition, answer and judgment duly certified by the clerk to be final and executory be lodged in the hands of the secretary of the Board of Liquidation of the City Debt of New Orleans, whose duty it shall be to record the same in a book kept for that purpose.

SEC. 147. [**Duty of the Board of Liquidation.**]—It shall be the duty of the Board of Liquidation to distribute the share of the funds provided for in Section 8 of Act 110 of 1890, which shall accrue to the School Board of the city of New Orleans, as follows, viz:

1. Out of the funds so accruing from the taxes for the years 1892, 1893 and 1894, it shall first pay to said School Board, in addition to amounts heretofore paid the sum of one hundred and sixty thousand dollars ($160,000).

2. Out of the funds so accruing from the taxes of the year 1895, it shall first pay to said School Board such an amount as will, with any amounts appropriated by the city of New Orleans for school purposes reach a total of two hundred and ninety-seven thousand five hundred dollars ($297,500).

3. Out of the funds so accruing from the taxes of the year 1896, and of each year thereafter, it shall first pay to said School Board for each year such an amount as will with any amounts appropriated by the city of New Orleans for school purposes reach a total of three hundred and thirty-seven thousand five hundred dollars ($337,500).

4. It shall, after making the payments aforesaid, distribute any amounts remaining in its hands and accruing to said School Board, among the holders of judgments so recorded with it, in the order of their registry until the same shall have been paid in full.

5. It shall pay over to said School Board any amounts accruing to it out of said funds after paying judgments in full.

SEC. 148. [City Treasurer, Ex-Officio School Treasurer.]—The treasurer of New Orleans shall ex-officio be the treasurer of said board and shall receive all funds apportioned by the State to such city, or received or collected for the support of the free public schools from any and all sources. He shall give bond, with good and solvent security, in the sum of ten thousand dollars ($10,000) in favor of the president of said board and his successors in office, to be accepted and approved by said board and recorded in the mortgage office of the parish, and which bond shall then be filed and kept on record in the office of the said board. The filing of said bond, and taking and filing the usual oath of office before any officer authorized to administer the same, shall qualify the treasurer to act.

SEC. 149. [Term of Office, Removal, Election of a Successor.]— Said treasurer shall hold his office for four years, or during his term of office as city treasurer, unless sooner removed after due trial and hearing by the said board, for neglect of duty or malfeasance in office; and in case of removal by the board, it shall elect a treasurer who shall not be a member. He shall receive the sum of six hundred dollars per annum for the trouble and expenses which may be incurred by him in the discharge of the duties imposed under this act, payable monthly on his own warrant, as hereinbefore provided for the payment of the superintendent's salary. He shall keep his office open at all such times as may be prescribed by said board, for the payment of pay-rolls or checks in favor of teachers and other employees of the board.

SEC. 150. [Ex-Officio Members of the City Board.]—The mayor, treasurer and comptroller of the city of New Orleans shall be ex-officio member of the said board and entitled to take part in all the debates and deliberations in said board on the ways and means for maintaining the public schools of said parish, but they shall not have the right to vote.

SEC. 151. [**Report of the Board.**]—In addition to the duties imposed upon boards of school directors, it shall be the duty of said board for the parish of Orleans to present to the Common Council of the city of New Orleans, on the first day of December of each year, a full report of the condition of the city schools, showing the number of teachers and other employees and their salaries; the number and location of school houses, with the condition thereof, and the estimated cost of keeping all appurtenant grounds in good repair during the ensuing year; also a detailed exhibit of all receipts and expenditures of the board for the schools during the previous twelve months; said report shall be accompanied with a statement certified by the officers of the board of the average daily attendance of pupils during the annual session, and the average expense per capita of their instruction.

SEC. 152. [**Budget of Expenses.**]—It shall be the duty of the Common Council of the city of New Orleans, in making up their budget of annual expenses, to include therein the amount necessary to meet the expenses of the schools, as shown by the statement of the actual attendance, and cost of instruction required by the preceding section, with such additional allowance for probable increased attendance and contingent expenses as may seem just and reasonable to the City Council, and to keep in good repair all school houses and school grounds belonging to the city; provided, that the sum appropriated with the probable receipts from the State school fund and poll tax shall not exceed the aggregate amount required for the maintenance of the schools during the year, and for the keeping in good repair all school houses and grounds belonging to the city, as shown by the statement of the school board; and, provided further, that the amount to be appropriated by said city shall not be less than the sum of $250,000; of said amount so to be appropriated by said City

Council, not less than \$175,000 shall be provided for the annual city budget of expenditure , and the balance out of the reserve fund of twenty per cent. constituted by Section 66 of Act No. 20, approved June 23d, 1882, and by Act No. 109, of 1886, and said balance is hereby constituted a first lien and claim against said reserve fund, and shall be paid out of the first collection made on account of the same and by preference over all claims whatsoever; provided further, that out of the amount so appropriated by said city, said board of directors shall, in the year eighteen hundred and eighty-nine (1889), and annually for five years thereafter, appropriate a sum sufficient to extinguish at least one-sixth of the unpaid claims against said board for the years 1880, 1881, 1882 and 1884, so that said claims shall be entirely paid by the beginning of the year 1895. The board of directors for the par sh of Orleans are hereby authorized to enforce the provisions of this section by the application to a court of competent jurisdiction, by a writ of mandamus or other effective remedy.*

SEC. 153. [Provisions for Affording Proper Evidences of Claims.] For the purpose of affording *proper evidence of said claims aforesaid (and for no other purposes whatsoever), said board shall issue certificates of indebtedness to an amount equal to the total amount of said claims and maturing in six equal installments on the first day of January, 1890, 1891, 1892, 1893, 1894 and 1895.

VIII. STATE SCHOOLS.

STATE NORMAL SCHOOL.
Act 73 *of* 1892.

154 (1) Object; to whom open
155. (2) Board of administrators; terms of office; successors.
156. (3) Powers of the board; appoint teachers; manage school finances; a body corporate; domicile.

157. (4) Meetings of the board; compensation.
158 (5) Faculty; their duties.
159. (6) Departments and classes.
160. (7) Qualifications for admission.
161. (*) Tuition free, except in certain instances.
162. (9) Diplomas equivalent to first grade teachers' certificates.

*The provisos of this section are declared unconstitutional by the Supreme Court. See abstract, "*Taxation*," from the 42d Annual in the Appendix of this book, case of *State ex rel School Board vs. City of New Orle ns.*

VIII. State Schools—Continued.

INDUSTRIAL SCHOOL AT RUSTON.

Act 68 of 1894.

163. (1) Object, location, proviso.
164. (2) Trustees: how appointed; vacancies, quorum.
165. (3) Trustees, a body corporate.
166. (4) Meetings.
167. (5) Branches to be taught.
168. (6) Faculty.
169. (7) State ownership of school property.

STATE UNIVERSITY.

Act 145 of 1877.

170. (1) Union of the State University and Agricultural and Mechanical College.
171. (2) Rights and privileges granted the two institutions, respectively, still in force.
172. (3) Object of the institution in literature, sciences, and arts.
173. (4) General education.
174. (5) Board of supervisors; seal; powers.
175. (6) Composition of the board; vacancies; how filled.
176. (7) Members of the board graduated by class for certain terms.
177. (8) Vice president; quorum.
178. (9) Regular and special meetings of the board.
179. (10) Officers of the board.
180. (11) President and faculty; salaries, duties and privileges.
181. (12) Branches to be taught.
182. (13) Affiliation of the university with other incorporated institutions.
183. (14) Course of study.
184. (15) Board to be charged with the purchase of necessary grounds.
185. (16) Power of the board to lease

the University's grounds in Rapides and Saint Bernard.
186. (17) Interest and income to be derived from the sale and lease of certain lands and property.
187. (18) Institution enjoined to teach agricultural and mechanical arts.
188. (20) The board to report to the Legislature.
189. (21) Powers and duties of the president of the University.
190. (22) Further powers of the president of the faculty.
191. (23) Grant, gift, devise, and bequest of property.
192. (24) Board to accept donations of property, etc.
193. (25) Authority of the board to invest funds.
194. (26) Construction to be placed upon donations.

Act 67 of 1860.

195. Military science to be taught.
196. Governor to issue commissions to the faculty.
197. Expenses of the board of supervisors.

Act 140 of 1880.

198. (1) Chairs in nautical instruction to be established.
199. (2) Governor requested to apply to the Secretary of the Navy for training ships, etc.

Act 100 of 1886.

200. (1) Beneficiary cadets—one allowed each parish and seventeen to the city of New Orleans.
201. (2) By whom and how appointed.
202. (4) Authority of the police juries and city council of New Orleans to appropriate funds

5

VIII. STATE SCHOOLS—Continued.

for the maintenance of beneficiary cadets.

203. (5) Conditions imposed upon
beneficiaries.

INSTITUTION FOR THE BLIND.

Act 92 *of* 1871.

204. (1) Establishment.
205. (2) Applicants, on what terms
admitted.
206. (3) Organization; terms of instruction.
207. (4) General control.
203. (5) First meeting.
209. (6) Residence, salary, and duties of principal.
210. (7) Duties of vice-president.
211. (8) Bond, duties, and salary of
the treasurer.
212. (9) By-laws and regulations.
213. (10) Industrial Home for the
Blind.
214. (11) Expenses of the board; how
paid.
215. (12) Admission regardless of
race.

INSTITUTION FOR THE DEAF AND
DUMB.

Act 88 *of* 1871.

216. (1) For the exclusive use of the
deaf and dumb.

217. (2) Admission of pupils.
218. (3) Literary and mechanical
education.
219. (4) Control, in whom vested.
220. (5) Officers.
221. (6) Duties of the superintendent.
222. (7) Duties of the treasurer.
223. (8) Rules and regulations; quorum.
224. (10) Expenses of members of the
board.

SOUTHERN UNIVERSITY.

(*For Persons of Color.*)

225. [*S*. 1, *A*. 87, 1880.]—Establishment
226. [*S*. 1, *A*. 65, 1882.]—Board of
trustees.
227. [*S*. 3, *A*. 87, 1880.]—Quorum.
228. [*S*. 4, A. 87, 1880.]—Officers of
the board; how elected; officers.
229. [*S*. 5, *A*. 87, 1880.]—Rules and
regulations; faculty.
230. [*S*. 6, A. 87, 1880.]—Powers of
the board of trustees.
231. [*S*. 1, *A*. 90, 1882.]—Faculty,
degrees, departments, and
courses.

STATE NORMAL SCHOOL.

SEC. 154. [Object—To Whom Open.]—The State Normal School, located at Natchitoches, in the parish of Natchitoches, in conformity with sections 4 and 8 of Act No. 51 of 1884, shall have far its object to train teachers for the public schools of Louisiana, and shall be open to white persons of either sex of age and qualifications as may be hereinafter prescribed.

SEC. 155. Board of Administrators—Terms of Office, Their Successors.—The board of administrators of said State Normal School shall consist of six competent white citizens, to be selected and appointed by the Governor of the State, one from the town of Natchitoches and from each of the first five circuits of the court of appeals. The Governor shall shall be, ex-officio, president of the board. The first board appointed under this act shall, at its first meeting, be divided by lot into three classes of two members each, the first class to hold office for two years, the second for four years, and the third for six years, from and after the first day of July, 1892. Their successors shall be appointed for the full term of six years. Vacancies caused by death or resignation shall be filled for the unexpired term by appointment of the Governor.

SEC. 156. [**Powers of the Board of Administrators.**]—The board of administrators shall elect all teachers employed in said State Normal School, determine their compensation, and manage the financial and other interests of the school. Said board shall be a body corporate with all the rights and powers of such bodies, and shall have its domicile at the town of Natchitoches, in the parish of Natchitoches.

SEC. 157. [**Meetings of the Board; Compensation.**]—Said board of administrators shall hold one regular meeting each year at the close of the annual session of the school. Special meetings may be called in such manner and held at such times as the board of administrators may determine. The members of said board of administrators shall receive no compensation for their services, except their actual traveling expenses and the per diem of members of the General Assembly while attending the sessions of the Board.

SEC. 158. [**The Faculty—Their Duties.**]—The faculty shall consist of a president, who shall be ex-officio a member of the board of administrators, and such additional instructors as the interests of the school may require. In addition to the regular work of the school, the faculty may be called upon to assist in the State Teachers' Institutes at such times and places as may be determined by the State Superintendent of Public Education and the President of the State Normal School.

SEC. 159. [Departments and Classes.]—The State Normal School shall contain two departments, the Normal Department and the Practice School. The Course of Study of the Normal Department may extend over a period of four years, and shall embrace thorough instruction and training in the history and science of education, the theory and practice of teaching, the organization and government of schools and such other branches of knowledge as may be deemed necessary to fit the students for the varied work of a complete system of public schools. The Practice School shall consist of such grades or classes, with such course of study, as the Board of Administrators may deem useful in giving the Normal students the necessary practice in the art of teaching.

SEC. 160. [Qualifications for Admission.]—Applicants for admission to the Normal Department must be at least fifteen years of age if female, and sixteen years of age if male; must give satisfactory evidence of good moral character and of requisite proficiency in the ordinary branches of a good common school education; and must declare in writing their full intention of continuing in the school until graduation, unless sooner discharged, and of teaching in the public schools of Louisiana for at least one year after graduation.

SEC. 161. [Tuition Free, Except in Some Instances.]—Tuition shall be free to all students of the Normal Department who fulfill all the requirements imposed by Section 160 of this Act, and to the pupils of the primary grades of the Practice School. All other students shall be charged such fees for tuition as may be prescribed by the board of administrators.

SEC. 162. [Diplomas.]—The board of administrators of the State Normal School is hereby empowered to confer diplomas upon all graduates of said school. This diploma shall entitle its holder to a first grade teacher's certificate, valid in any town or parish of the State for four years from the date of graduation, at the expiration of which time it may be renewed, for the same period, by the State Board of Education, upon satisfactory evidence of the ability, progress and moral character of the teacher making application for such renewal. Furthermore, the diploma of the State Normal School shall entitle its holder to such degree of preference in the selection of teachers for the public schools of the State as may be deemed wise and expedient by the State Board of Education.

INDUSTRIAL INSTITUTE AND COLLEGE.

SEC. 163. [Industrial College—Object, Location, Privilege.]—An Industrial Institute and College is hereby established for the education of the white children of the State of Louisiana in the arts and sciences. Said Institute shall be known as "The Industrial Institute and College of Louisiana," and shall be located at Ruston, Lincoln parish, La., provided said town and parish shall donate ten thousand dollars ($10,000) to said Institute, and the same shall be organized as hereinafter provided.

SEC. 164. [Trustees—How Appointed; Vacancies, Quorum.]—The Governor of the State shall nominate and appoint, by and with the advice and consent of the Senate, one person from each Congressional District of this State and two from the State at large, to be trustees and to serve as such for four years. Immediately after they shall be assembled, in consequence of their first appointment, they shall be divided by lot into two equal classes, so that the term of three of those appointed from the Congressional Districts and one appointed from the State at large, shall expire in two years and the term of the other half shall expire in four years from the date of their appointment, so that one-half may be chosen every two years. Vacancies shall be filled as in case of other offices in this State. The Governor shall be ex-officio a member of said board of trustees and shall, when present, act as president of the board, but the board shall elect one of their number as vice-president. Five of the trustees shall constitute a quorum for the transaction of business.

SEC. 165. [Trustees, a Body Corporate.]—The board of trustees of said institute and college, be and the same are hereby declared a body politic and corporate, shall be domiciled at Ruston, La., shall have a seal, shall sue and be sued, contract and be contracted with, may hold, purchase, sell and convey property, whether movable or immovable, which may be necessary or beneficial in carrying out the purposes of this act. Said board of trustees may provide under proper regulations and rules for conferring degrees and awarding diplomas and granting certificates, as rewards and honors for learning and skill, to the pupils of said institute.

SEC. 166. [Meetings of the Trustees.—Said board of trustees shall fix the time or times for regular meetings and may be convened at any time the Governor as ex-officio president may deem it expedient to do so, in order to transact business connected with said institute and college. The president of the faculty and teachers shall be secretary of the board of trustees, and he shall keep in a well bound book, a record of all the proceedings had by said board, and his compensation for this service shall be fixed by the board; provided, that said board may elect a suitable person as secretary pro tem to act until the institute be put in operation.

SEC. 167. [Branches to be Taught.]—The said board of trustees shall possess all the power necessary and proper for the accomplishment of the trust reposed in them, viz: The establishment of a first-class Industrial Institute and College for the education of the white children of Louisiana in the arts and sciences, at which such children may acquire a thorough academic and literary education, together with a knowledge of kindergarten instruction, of telegraphy, stenography and photography, of drawing, painting, designing and engraving in their industrial application; also a knowledge of fancy, practical and general needle work; also a knowledge of book-keeping and agricultural and mechanical arts, together with such other practical industries as from time to time may be suggested to them by experience, or such as will tend to promote the general object of said institute and college to-wit: Fitting and preparing such children, male and female, for the practical industries of the age.

SEC. 168. [Faculty.]—The board of trustees shall select and appoint a president and the professors of said Institute and College, and such other officers as they may deem necessary to put and maintain the same in successful operation, and shall make such rules and regulations for the government of said officers as they may deem advisable; they shall prescribe such a course of discipline as may be necessary to enforce the faithful discharge of the duties of all officers, professors and students. They shall prescribe the course or courses of instruction so as to secure a thorough education and the best possible instruction in all of said industrial studies, and they shall adopt all such by-laws and regulations as they may deem necessary to carry out all the purposes and objects of said institution.

SEC. 169. [State Ownership of College Property.]—All the property acquired in any way by said board of trustees shall really be the property of and belonging to the State of Louisiana, but shall be held, controlled and managed by said board of trustees for the benefit of the said Industrial Institute and College.

THE LOUISIANA STATE UNIVERSITY AND AGRICULTURAL AND MECHANICAL COLLEGE.

SEC. 170. [Union of the State University and the Agricultural and Mechanical College.]—The Louisiana State University, as now established and located at Alexandria, in the parish of Rapides, and the Louisiana State Agricultural and Mechanical College, as now established and located in the parish of St. Bernard, be and they are hereby united and constituted into one and the same institution of learning, which shall hereafter be known and designated under the name and title of the Louisiana State University and Agricultural and Mechanical College, and said institution of learning, the Louisiana State University and Agricultural and Mechanical College, as hereby created, shall be established temporarily at Baton Rouge, in the parish of East Baton Rouge.

SEC. 171. [Rights and Privileges Granted the Two Institutions Respectively, Still in Force.]—All legal rights and privileges, as granted by the Congress of the United States and the Legislature of Louisiana, and all the legal obligations and requirements, as imposed by congressional and legislative enactments, and binding upon the two institutions of learning respectively, which have been in the preceding section united and constituted into one and the same institution of learning, shall be of full force and effect with and upon the Louisiana State University and Agricultural and Mechanical College, as hereinbefore constituted and established; excepting such legal rights, privileges, obligations, and requirements as may be specifically repealed by the provisions of this act.

SEC. 172. [Object of the Institution.]—The Louisiana State University and Agricultural and Mechanical College, as hereinbefore created, shall have for its object to become an institution of learning, in the broadest and highest sense, where literature, science and all the arts may be taught; where the principles of truth and honor may be established, and a noble sense of personal and patriotic and religious duty inculcated; in fine, to fit the citizen to perform justly, skillfully, and magnanimously all the offices, both private and public, of peace and war.

SEC. 173. [General Instruction.]—The Louisiana State University and Agricultural and Mechanical College, as hereinbefore created, shall provide general instruction and education in all the departments of literature, science, art, and industrial and professional pursuits; and it shall provide special instruction for the purpose of agriculture, the mechanic arts, mining, military science and art, civil engineering, law, medicine, commerce and navigation.

SEC. 174. [Board of Supervisors.]—The Louisiana State University and Agricultural and Mechanical College, as hereinbefore created, constituted and established, shall be under the direction and control of fifteen supervisors, who shall be a body corporate, under the style and title of the board of supervisors of the Louisana State University and Agricultural and Mechanical College, with the right, as such, to use a common seal, and who shall be capable in law to receive all donations, subscriptions, and bequests, in trust for said University and Agricultural and Mechanical College, and to recover all debts which may become the property of said University and Agricultural and Mechanical College, and to sue and be sued in courts of justice, and in general to do all acts for the benefit of the Louisiana State University and Agricultural and Mechanical College, which are incident to bodies corporate.

SEC. 175. [Composition of the Board.]—The Governor of the the State shall be ex officio president of the board of supervisors, and the State Superintendent of Public Education and the president of the faculty of the university shall be members ex-officio of said board, and the twelve remaining members shall be appointed by the Governor by and with the advice and consent of the Senate; provided, that three of the said twelve remaining members shall have been students of the Louisiana State University, as it existed prior to the passage of this act, and have taken degrees and be titled graduates of said institution; and provided further, that only one member shall be appointed from any one parish, except the parish of Orleans, from which two members shall be appointed; and also further provided, that one of the twelve members to be appointed by the Governor shall reside in the parish of East Baton Rouge, in which, as hereinbefore provided, the Louisiana State University and Agricultural and Mechanical College has been, temporarily, established and located. And whenever a vacancy occurs in the board of supervisors, for any cause, the same shall be filled for the unexpired term in the same manner.

SEC. 176. [How the Supervisors are Appointed.]—Three of the twelve members of the board of supervisors to be appointed by the Governor in accordance with the provisions of the foregoing section of this act, shall be commissioned and hold their offices for one year, three for two years, three for three years, and three for four years. Their successors snall be appointed in like manner, and shall hold their offices for the full term of four years, from the first day of January next succeeding their appointments. and until their successors are appointed and qualified.

SEC. 177. [Vice-President of the Board; Quorum.]—The member of the board of supervisors appointed for the parish of East Baton Rouge, in which, as hereinbefore provided, the Louisiana State University and Agricultural and Mechanical College has been temporarily established and located, shall be ex-officio the vice-president of the board, to preside over the meetings of the board in the absence of the Governor. Five members of the board of supervisors, including the president or vice-president shall constitute a quorum for the transaction of business; provided, that all of the acts of the said such five members, at such meeting, shall be submitted for ratification or rejection at the next meeting of the board of supervisors, when a majority of all the fourteen members of the board may be present.

SEC. 178. [Meetings of the Board—When Held.]—There shall be four regular stated meetings of the board of supervisors, at the university, in each and every year; one the first Monday in April, another on the Monday before the close of the annual session of the university, which shall be July 4; another on Monday before the opening of the annual session of the university, which shall be October 5; and another on the first Monday in December; special meetings of the board of supervisors shall be called in such manner and held at such other times and places as the Governor of the State or the board of supervisors may determine.

SEC. 179. [Officers of the Board.]—The board of supervisors shall, at their first meeting, elect a secretary, who shall record, attest and preserve their proceedings; and a treasurer, who shall give bond for the faithful performance of his duties, and in such sum as shall be determined by the board; provided, that the treasurer shall not be a member of the board of supervisors, nor a professor or other officer, or other employe of the university; and provided further, that the treasurer shall never be interested, directly or indirectly, in any contract for furnishing supplies or articles of any kind to the university, or have any business transactions with, or on account of the university that tend, directly or indirectly, to his own personal profits; nor shall any money ever be paid to the treasurer in his personal capacity, or on account of the university, except what may be his salary or compensation as treasurer.

SEC. 180. [Faculty—Salary, Duties and Privileges.]—The board of supervisors shall have the power to engage a president and other professors, and all other officers necessary for conducting the literary, scientific, military, and technical departments, and all the financial and civil concerns and interest of the university, and to remove and displace the same at pleasure; to fix and regulate the salaries of the professors and all other offices, and to determine all other changes, excepting that there shall be no fee for tuition or for the use of the library, apparatus, laboratory, cabinets, museum, workshop, experimental farm, or other educational appliances charged to any student or cadet; to establish rules for the good government and discipline of the students or cadets; to prescribe the duties of all officers, employes, servants and others; to confer diplomas upon the recommendation of the president and faculty, on students for proficiency in any branch of literature or science, or department of learning, and, in general, to make all rules and regulations which may be deemed necessary for the proper government of the university and for promoting the objects for which it has been founded. But nothing in this act shall be construed as obligating the State to pay any debt contracted by the board of supervisors in case it should, at any time, exceed the appropriation made for the institution; nor shall any of the property of the university ever be seized and sold to pay any debt of the institution, by virtue of any decree of court. The title to all property owned and held by the Louisiana State University and Agricultural and Mechanical College is hereby declared to vest in the State of Louisiana.

SEC. 181. [**Branches to be Taught.**]—There shall be maintained in the Louisiana State University and Agricultural and Mechanical College, as hereinbefore constituted and established:

First—Schools of literature, including the languages of the principal nations of ancient and modern times, philosophy, logic, rhetoric and elocution, history, ethics, metaphysics and such other and special branches of learning as the board of supervisors may determine.

Second—Schools of science, including mathematics, astronomy, engineering, architecture, drawing, physics, chemistry, botany, zoology, agriculture, mechanics, mining, navigation and commerce, and such other special branches of learning as the board of supervisors may determine.

Third—Schools of the useful and fine arts, and of military science and art.

Fourth—Schools of medicine and law.

Fifth—Such other schools as the board of supervisors may establish.

SEC. 182. [**Affiliation With Any Incorporated Institution.**]— The board of supervisors may affiliate with the Louisiana State University and Agricultural and Mechanical College any incorporated university or college, or school of medicine, law or other special course of instruction, upon such terms as may be deemed expedient; and such university, college or school may retain the control of its own property, have its own board of trustees, faculties and president respectively; and the students of such universities, colleges or schools recommended by the respective faculties thereof, may receive from the Louisiana State University and Agricultural and Mechanical College, the degrees of those universities, colleges or schools, and the said students of learning or special schools, thus graduated, shall rank as graduates of the Louisiana State University and Agricultural and Mechanical College.

SEC. 183. [**Course of Study.**]—It shall be the duty of the board of supervisors, immediately after its organization, to prescribe, in detail, the course of studies, both theoretical and practical, to be pursued at the University and Agricultural and Mechanical College, and to draw up a project of the system of instruction so adopted.

SEC. 184. [Board to Purchase Grounds Necessary for the University.)—The board of supervisors shall be charged with the purchase of all necessary grounds and lands for the purpose of the University and Agricultural and Mechanical College, and with the purchase or erection, or both, as may be necessary, of all requisite buildings, workshops, laboratories and other fixtures and contrivances needed for the academic, military, industrial or other departments of the University and Agricultural and Mechanical College, and with the purchase of all necessary supplies or articles for the use of the University and Agricultural and Mechanical College; provided, that no member of the board of supervisors shall have any personal interest in any contract, or purchase, or sales, or in any business transaction of any kind whatever, for or on account of said University and Agricultural and Mechanical College; and said board of supervisors shall be charged with the care and preservation of all the buildings, grounds and appurtenances of the University, after they shall have been provided.

SEC. 185. [Power of the Board to Lease Certain Lands in Rapides and Saint Bernard.]—The board of supervisors be, and they are hereby empowered to lease, as early as may be practicable, and invest the proceeds thereof in the stocks of the State of Louisiana, or in the stocks of the United States, all the buildings and grounds and lands belonging to and held by the Louisiana State University, as it was established and located in the parish of Rapides prior to the passage of this act and to sell or lease all the buildings and grounds and land belonging to and held by the Louisiana Agricultural and Mechanical College, as it was established and located in the parish of Saint Bernard prior to the passage of this act; and said stocks or bonds shall be deposited for safe keeping with the Treasurer of the State.

SEC. 186. [Income from Congressional Grants.]—For the endowment, support, and maintenance of the Louisiana State

University, as heretofore created, constituted, and established, there shall be and is hereby inviolably appropriated and placed at the disposal of the supervisors thereof, to be drawn from the State treasurer, upon the order of the president of the board, made upon the Auditor of the State, countersigned by the secretary of the board, and payable to the order of the treasurer of the board of supervisors, all the interest and income derived and to be derived from the sales of all lands granted, or that hereafter may be granted, to the State of Louisiana by the United States, for the use of a seminary of learning, and all the interest and income of the fund derived and to be derived from the sales of all land and land scrip granted, or that may hereafter be granted to the State of Louisiana by virtue of an act of Congress, entitled, "An act donating lands to the several States and Territories, which may provide colleges for the benefit of agriculture and the mechanic arts," approved July 2, 1862; and all the interest and income of the funds to be derived from the lease of the buildings, grounds and lands in the parish of Rapides, and owned by or held for the use of the Louisiana State University, as it existed prior to the passage of this act; and from the sale or lease of the buildings, grounds, and lands in the parish of Saint Bernard, owned by or held for the use of the Louisiana Agricultural and Mechanical College, as it existed prior to the passage of this act; and all such gifts, grants, contributions and other donations to the endowment thereof, as may be derived from any and all sources.

SEC. 187. [Instruction in Agricultural and Mechanic Arts.]— It is particularly enjoined upon the board of supervisors of this University and Agricultural and Mechanical College to make the training in those branches of study relating to agriculture and the mechanic arts as practical as possible, and to that end to provide the necessary workshops and laboratories, and to secure suitable land in the vicinity of the University and Agricultural and Mechanical College for an experimental farm. For the purchase of an experimental farm the board of supervisors is hereby authorized to expend a sum not exceeding the amount specified in the act of Congress hereinbefore mentioned, viz: ten per cent upon the amount received by the State, as the proceeds of the sale of the lands and the land scrip donated by the general government of the United States.

SEC. 188. [Report of the Board of Supervisors.]—At the regular stated meeting in December of each and every year, the board of supervisors shall, through the Governor of the State, make a report in detail to the Legislature, showing the true condition and wants of the University and Agricultural and Mechanical College, and recording any improvements and experiments made in agriculture and the mechanic arts, with their costs and results, the names of the professors and students, the amount of receipts and disbursements, together with the nature, costs and results of all important scientific investigations and experiments in the useful arts, and such other matters, including State, industrial and commercial statistics, and literary, historical, philological and philosophical discussions or essays as may be deemed important or useful; one copy of which shall be transmitted to all the other colleges which shall be endowed under the provisions of the act of Congress of July 2d, 1862, as hereinbefore mentioned.

SEC. 189. [Powers of the President of the Institution.]—The president of the Louisiana State University and Agricultural and Mechanical College shall be the president of the faculty of professors thereof, and executive head of the institution in all its departments. As such officer, he shall have authority, subject to the board of supervisors, to give general direction to the practical affairs and scientific investigations of the University and Agricultural and Mechanical College, and in the recess of the board of supervisors, to remove any employe or subordinate officer not a member of the faculty, and supply for the time any vacancies thus created; and so long as the interests of the institution require it, he shall be charged with the duties of one of the professorships; and it shall be the duty of the president of the University and Agricultural and Mechanical College to make

to the State Superintendent of Public Education, on or before
the first Monday in December in each year, and every year, a
report, in detail, showing the progress and condition of the
university, the names of the professors and students, the nature,
costs and results of all important investigations and experiments,
and such other matters, including industrial, economical philosophical, and educational statistics as he shall deem useful.

SEC. 190. [**Further Powers of the President of the University.**]
The president of the University and Agricultural and Me
chanical College shall be specially charged with the discipline
of the University and Agricultural and Mechanical College, and
be held directly responsible for the good order of the establishment, and especially for the conduct and behavior of the students
or cadets. And it is hereby declared not to be the intent of this
act to devolve in any way upon the professors, as such, or upon
the faculty of professors, the maintenance of good order and
discipline among the students or cadets, or to hold them responsible for the conduct or behavior of the cadets or students outside their class or lecture rooms and during the time of recitation,
or study, or lecture; and it is particularly enjoined upon the
board of supervisors to delegate to the president of the University and Agricultural and Mechanical College, and through
him, to such assistant disciplinarians as may be assigned him
from among the professors and assistant professors, sufficient
authority to enable him to maintain proper discipline and good
order, and to meet promptly and efficiently the great responsibility hereby imposed on him. No student or cadet shall ever
be tried by the faculty of professors, or by any committee oi
professors, for any breach of discipline or other misconduct.
But no provision of this section, or this act, shall be construed as militating against a proper subordination of professors or other officers to the president of the University
and Agricultural and Mechanical College, and the necessity of obeying all the rules and orders which he may impose on them in virtue of the provisions of this act, and of
the rightful authority delegated to him by the board of super-

visors, as hereby enjoined upon the board; and the president of the University and Agricultural and Mechanical College shall have the power to assemble the faculty or any committee or num ber of the professors at any time he may see fit, for consultation or advice or other action, or any subject matter he may choose to lay before them; provided only, that in all matters of discipline and relating to the conduct and behavior of students or cadets the president alone, and not the faculty or any professor, shall decide and act.

SEC. 191. [Grant, Gift, Devise, and Bequest of Property to the Institution.]—The State of Louisiana, in its corporate capacity, may take by grant, gift, devise, or bequest, any property for the use of the Louisiana State University and Agricultural and Mechanical College, and hold the same, and apply the funds arising therefrom, through the board of supervisors, for the support of said institution of learning.

SEC. 192. [Board May Accept Donations, Etc.]—The board of supervisors, in its corporate capacity, may take by grant, gift, devise or bequest, any property for the use of the Louisiana State University and Agricultural and Mechanical College, or any school thereof, or of any professorship, chair, or scholarship therein, or for the library, museum, observatory, workshops, experimental farm, apparatus, cabinet, or for any purpose appropriate to the University and Agricultural and Mechanical College; and such property shall be taken, received, held, managed, and invested, and the proceeds thereof used, bestowed and applied by the said board of supervisors, for the purposes, provisions and conditions prescribed by the respective grant, gift, devise or bequest, and in accordance with the provisions of sections 174, 180 and 186.

SEC. 193. [Investment of Permanent Funds.]—The board of supervisors may invest any of the permanent funds of the Louisiana State University and Agricultural and Mechanical College which are now, or may hereafter be, in its custody, in productive, unincumbered real estate in this State, subject to the power of the Legislature to control or change such investments, excepting such as by the provisions of previous sections of this act, or by the terms of their acquisition, must be otherwise invested.

SEC. 194. [Construction to be Placed Upon Donations.]—If by the terms of any grant, gift, devise or bequest, such as are hereinbefore described in sections 191 and 192, conditions are imposed which are impracticable under the provisions of the Revised Statutes of this State, such grants, gifts, devise, or bequest shall not thereby fail, but such conditions shall be rejected and the intent of the donor carried out as near as may be.

SEC. 195. [Instruction in Military Science.]—In the course of study pursued at the University, the board of supervisors shall cause instruction to be given in the military branches of science. The students shall be styled cadets, and shall form a military corps, under the command of the president and such other professors as may be assigned to that branch of instruction. They shall constitute a guard for all public property, arms, or munitions now there or which may hereafter be assembled there; and the president shall receipt for all such property, arms or munitions, and shall obey all orders relative to their preservation or delivery that he may receive from the Governor of the State.

SEC. 196. [Governor to Issue Commissions to Professors.]— The Governor of the State shall cause to be issued to the president of the Louisiana State University a commission as colonel, and to such other professors as may be assigned to command commissions as majors, captains and lieutenants, according to the strength of the command; provided, that such commissions shall not entitle the holders to any rank in the militia of the State, or to any claim whatever to compensation other than that attached to their positions as professors.

SEC. 197. [Expenses of the Supervisors.]—The reasonable expenses of the supervisors, in going to, and attending, the meetings of the board, shall be paid by the State; and it shall be the duty of the board of directors to set forth in their annual report the amount of such expenses, which amount shall be paid by the State Treasurer, on the warrant of the Auditor, who shall issue the said warrant upon the certificate of the president or vice-president of the said board; provided, however, that the said amount does not exceed $250 in any one year.   •

SEC. 198. [**Nautical Instruction.**]—The board of administrators of the University of Louisiana, at New Orleans, and the board of supervisors of the Louisiana State University and Agricultural and Mechanical College, at Baton Rouge, be and are hereby authorized to establish chairs of nautical education at said institutions, under the provisions of acts of Congress on the subject of nautical education in the several ports of the Union.

SEC. 199. [**Governor Instructed to Apply to the Government for Training Ships, Etc.**]—The Governor of the State of Louisiana is hereby instructed to apply to the Secretary of the Navy for the suitable vessels, apparel, charts, books, instruments of navigation, etc., for that purpose immediately upon the establishment of said chairs in said universities.

SEC. 200. [**Beneficiary Cadets.**]—Each parish, as now created or that may hereafter be created in the State, shall have the right to delegate to the Louisiana State University and Agricultural and Mechanical College one beneficiary cadet, and the city of New Orleans shall have the right to delegate to said institution seventeen beneficiary cadets; or one from each ward of said city, said beneficiaries to remain at said institution four years, • unless sooner graduated or otherwise discharged; provided, that no beneficiary cadet shall be permitted to resign from said institution, without the consent of the board of supervisors thereof, which consent shall be given only in a case of urgent necessity, such as serious and long protracted ill health, duly declared by the certificate of the surgeon of said institution, or other competent physician, be of such a nature as to render it impossible for said cadet to pursue his studies with advantage.

SEC. 201. [**Police Juries and City Council to Elect Beneficiaries.**]—The police jury of each parish and the city council of New Orleans, respectively, may, at a regular meeting, elect the number of beneficiary cadets to which said parish or city is entitled as aforesaid, of such age and qualifications as may be prescribed by the board of supervisors for admission to the college classes of said University and Agricultural and Mechanical College; and shall cause the beneficiary so selected to report in person at said institution on or before said 5th day of October; provided, that said beneficiary cadets shall be selected from the number of those residents of said parish or of said city, who have not themselves, nor have their parents, the means of defraying the whole of their necessary expenses of maintenance and support at said institution, which facts shall be duly certified to the president of said institution, by the president of said police jury, or said city council of New Orleans, as true, to the best of his knowledge and belief.

SEC. 202. [**Authority of the Police Juries and City Council of New Orleans to Appropriate Funds for Beneficiaries.**]—For maintenance and board of said beneficiaries in said institution, the police juries of the several parishes and the city council of the city of New Orleans, be and are hereby authorized and empowered to appropriate out of their respective treasuries, a sufficient sum to defray the necessary expenses of said cadets as appointed under the provisions of this act; provided, that the expense of no cadet shall exceed two hundred and fifty dollars ($250) per annum; provided, that under no circumstances shall any part of this sum be paid by the State.

SEC. 203. [**Conditions to the Benefit of Scholarships.**]—In order to take advantage of the right granted to each parish and to the city of New Orleans, in section 200 of this act, each parish and city shall make an appropriation of $150 per annum out of any money in its treasury for the maintenance and board in said institution of each beneficiary cadet delegated by said parish or said city, said sum to be paid to the treasurer of such institution before the admission of said cadet; and the power to make such appropriation is hereby granted to the police juries of the several parishes and to the city council of New Orleans.

INSTITUTION FOR THE BLIND.

SEC. 204. [Establishment of the Institution at Baton Rouge.]—An institution for the instruction of the blind exclusively be and the same is hereby established at the city of Baton Rouge, in this State.

SEC. 205. [Applicants—On What Terms Admitted.]—All blind persons, residents of this State, of sound mind and good moral character, shall be entitled to admission into said institution as pupils, and shall be provided with instruction, board, lodging, medicine and medical attendance at the expense of the institution, and all those whose indigent circumstances shall be shown by the certificate of any member of the police jury of the parish, or by the mayor of the town or city where they reside, and such only, shall be furnished with clothing at the expense of the institution.

SEC. 206. [Organization of the Institution and Instruction.]—The institution shall be thoroughly organized in its academic, musical, and mechanical departments, and every pupil shall receive such instruction as it can afford and the capacity of the pupil will permit. All persons admitted as pupils, between the ages of eight and fourteen years, may continue in the institution nine years; all admitted between the ages of fourteen and seventeen years, may continue six years, and all admitted at an age exceeding seventeen years may continue four years as pupils.

SEC. 207. [General Control.]—The general control of said institution shall be vested in a board of trustees, to be composed of the Governor of the State, who shall be ex-officio president of the board, the principal of the institution, and five members to be appointed for the term of four years by the Governor, by and with the advice and consent of the Senate. Said board is hereby declared a body politic and corporate in deed and in law, and shall have full power to sue and be sued, and to make contracts, and to acquire and hold by purchase or donation any real or personal estate necessary for the uses of said institution. The domicile of said corporation is established at Baton Rouge, and the vice-president of the board shall be the officer upon whom all legal process shall be served to bind said board.

SEC. 208. [**First Meeting.**]—The first meeting of the board of trustees shall be held at such a time and place as may be fixed by the Governor, and they shall at said meeting elect a principal for the institution, a vice-president of the board, a treasurer and such other officers as may be necessary for the proper organization and management of the institution.

SEC. 209. [**Residence, Salary and Duties of Principal.**]—The principal shall have the charge and management of the institution; he shall reside in the institution, and receive such salary and perform such duties as may be determined by the board.

SEC. 210. [**Duties of the Vice-President.**]—The vice-president shall preside at the meetings of the board in the absence of the president, and shall exercise a general supervision over the affairs of the institution.

SEC. 211. [**Treasurer.**]—The treasurer shall give bond in such sum as the board of trustees may determine, with security to the satisfaction of the vice-president. He shall receive from the State Treasurer the appropriations which may from time to time be made by the Legislature for the support of the institution, upon his warrant, countersigned by the Governor. He shall pay out the same upon the order of the principal of the institution, countersigned by the vice-president of the board. He shall receive such salary as may be determined by the board, and both he and the principal may be removed at their pleasure.

SEC. 212. [**By-Laws and Regulations.**]—The board of trustees shall have power to make all needful rules and regulations for the government of said institution and also all needful rules and regulations for the government of the industrial home for the blind, hereinafter provided for. Three members of the board shall constitute a quorum for the transaction of business.

SEC. 213. [**Industrial Home for the Blind.**]—There shall be attached to said institution, and under the control of the board of trustees thereof, an industrial home, in which shall be received blind persons, residents of the State of Louisiana, who are of sound mind and good moral character. The inmates of this home shall be provided with board and lodging, and furnished with work at the trade or trades introduced therein; they shall receive wages for their work, and be required to pay for their support. Any properly qualified person desiring admission into the home, who has not learned any trade wrought at therein, may be admitted and receive support and instruction in some trade for one year. If, at the end of that time, it shall appear that such person is unable or unwilling to learn a trade, he shall not be entitled to longer residence in the home, the true intent and purpose of this act being to provide a shop and residence for industrious blind persons, and to furnish them an opportunity to escape pauperism and mendicancy, and not to establish an alms-house.

SEC. 214. [**Expenses of the Board of Trustees.**]—The expenses of the board of trustees, incurred in attending the meetings of the board, shall be paid out of the funds of the institution.

SEC. 215. [**Admission Regardless of Race.**]—No part of this act shall be construed so as to deprive any person on account of race or color of the privilege of admittance into the institution.

INSTITUTION FOR THE DEAF AND DUMB.

SEC. 216. [**Institution for the Exclusive Use of the Deaf and Dumb.**]—The institution heretofore known as the Louisiana Institution for the Deaf and Dumb and the Blind, located at Baton Rouge, in this State, be and the same is hereby reorganized by the provisions of this act for the exclusive benefit of the deaf and dumb.

SEC. 217. [**Admission of Pupils.**]—All the deaf and dumb residents of this State of sound mind and proper health of body, and between the ages of eight and twenty-five, shall be admitted to said institution as pupils, and be provided with instruction, board, lodging, medicine, and medical attendance at the expense of the institution, and all those in such indigent circumstances as shall appear by the certificate of any member of the police jury of the parish, or the mayor of the city where they reside, to render such aid necessary, shall also be furnished with clothing and traveling expenses to and from the institutions.

SEC. 218. [**Literary and Mechanical Education.**]—The institution shall afford all requisite facilities for providing a good literary education and a mechanical department in which instruction shall be given in such trades as may be best suited to render the pupils self-sustaining citizens.

SEC. 219. [**Control—In Whom Vested.**]—The general control or said institution shall be vested in a board of trustees, to be composed of the Governor of the State, who shall be ex-officio president of the board, the superintendent of the institution, and five members, to be appointed by the Governor, by and with the advice and consent of the Senate. Said board is hereby declared to be a body politic and corporate in deed and in law, and shall have full power to sue and be sued, to make contracts, and to acquire and hold, by purchase or donation, any real or personal estate, as may be necessary for the uses of said institution. The domicile of said corporation is established at Baton Rouge, and the vice-president of the board shall be the officer upon whom all legal process shall be served to bind said board.

SEC. 220. [**Officers.**]—The first meeting of the board of trustees shall be held at such time and place as may be fixed by the Governor, and they shall, at said meeting, elect a superintendent for the institution, a vice-president of the board, a treasurer, and such other officers as may be necessary for the proper organization and management of the institution.

SEC. 221. [**Duties of the Superintendent.**]—The superintendent shall have charge and management of the institution; he shall reside in the institution, and receive such salary and perform such duties as may be determined by the board.

SEC. 222. [**Duties of the Treasurer.**]—The treasurer shall give bond in such sum as the board of trustees may determine, with security to the satisfaction of the vice-president. He shall receive from the State Treasurer the appropriation made from time to time by the Legislature for the support of the institution, upon his warrant, countersigned by the Governor. He shall pay out the same upon the order of the superintendent of the institution, countersigned by the vice-president. He shall receive such salary as may be determined by the board, and both he and the superintendent may be removed by the board for any good cause.

SEC. 223. [**Quorum and Rules of the Board.**]—The board of trustees shall have the power to make all needful rules and regulations for the government of said institution, and three members shall constitute a quorum for the transaction of business. In the absence of the president the vice-president shall act as president of the board.

SEC. 224. [**Expenses of Trustees—How Paid.**]—The expenses of the members of the board of trustees, incurred in attending the meetings of the board, shall be paid out of the funds of the institution.

THE SOUTHERN UNIVERSITY.

(For Persons of Color.)

SEC. 225. [**Establishment.**]—There shall be established in the city of New Orleans a university for the education of persons of color, to be named and entitled the "Southern University."

SEC. 226. [**Board of Trustees.**]—The said university shall be governed and directed by a board of trustees, to be composed of twelve members, who shall be appointed by the Governor by and with the advice and consent of the Senate; provided, that at least four of said board of twelve shall be appointed from the colored race; vacancies shall be filled in a similar manner. The members of the board shall be appointed to serve during four years, but any member failing to attend two successive regular meetings of the board shall, except in case of sickness or other good cause, be considered no longer a member of said board, and the Governor, on receiving official notice of such absence from the president of the board, whose duty it shall be to report the same, shall immediately fill the vacancy in the manner prescribed.

SEC. 227. [Quorum.]—Six members of said board, at a stated or regularly called session, shall constitute a quorum.

SEC. 228. [Officers of the Board—How Elected, Duties.]— The said board of trustees shall be empowered to elect from among their own members a president and vice-president of the board, a secretary and treasurer; the treasurer shall give bond in the sum of ten thousand dollars for the faithful perform- ance of his duties, and shall pay out money only upon warrants issued by the president of the board, countersigned by the presi- dent of the faculty; provided, that the treasurer shall not be a professor or other officer or employe of the university, and shall not be interested, directly or indirectly, in any contract for fur- nishing supplies or articles of any kind to the university; pro- vided further, that at the discretion of the board the two offices of secretary and treasurer may be combined in one person.

SEC. 229. [Rules and Regulations; Faculty.]—The said board of trustees shall be empowered to enact general rules and by-laws for the said university in all its departments, and to elect a president of the faculty, professors and teachers, and determine their compensation; also, all officers and employes that may be necessary, and prescribe their duties and compensation.

SEC. 230. [Powers of the Board of Trustees.]—The said de- partment shall be organized as a corporation under the general laws of the State of Louisiana, and the trustees thereof shall be capable in law to receive all donations, trusts and bequests made to the "Southern University," and manage the same, to sue and be sued in courts of justice, and to do all other acts in the prem- ises incident to such trustees.

SEC. 231. [Faculty, Degrees, Departments, and Courses.]— There shall be established by said board of trustees a faculty of arts and letters, which shall be competent to instruct in every branch of a liberal education, and under rules of, and in concur- rence with, the board of trustees, to graduate students and grant all degrees appertaining to letters and arts known to universities and colleges in Europe and America, on persons competent and deserving the same.

There may also be established by said board of trustees a department of law and medicine. The department of law shall consist of three (3) or more learned professors, learned and skilled in the practice of law in this State, who shall be required to a full course of lectures on international, constitutional, commercial and municipal or civil law and instruction in the practice thereof. The medical department of the university shall consist of not less than three professors. They shall be appointed by the board of trustees from regular practicing physicians of the State. The degree of bachelor of law and doctor of medicine, granted by them, shall authorize the person upon whom it is conferred to practice physic and surgery in this State.

IX. Tulane University of Louisiana.

Act No. 43 of 1884 and Amendment to the Constitution.

232. (1) Board of Administrators.

233. (2) Rights, powers, privileges, franchises and immunities of the board.

234. (3) Power to hold and own property, real and personal.

235. (4) Name of the university to be the Tulane University of Louisiana of Louisiana—its powers, privileges, immunities and franchises.

236. (5) Exemption from taxation.

237. (6) Transfer of rights, powers, etc., from the University of Louisiana to the Administrators of the Tulane Education Fund; Scholarships

238. (7) The act declared to be a contract between the State and the Administrators of the Tulane Education Fund.

Laws Governing the "University of Louisiana" Applicable to the Tulane University of Louisiana.

239. [S. 1352, R. S.]—Corporate powers of the board of administrators.

240. [S. 1353, R. S.]—Departments of the University.

241. [1354, R. S.]—Powers of the board of administrators.

242. [S. 1358, R. S.]—By-laws and regulations.

243. [S. 1359, R. S.]—Literary honors and degrees.

244. [S 1368, R. S.]—Transfer of property.

245. [S. 1369, R. S.]—Law department.

246. [S. 1370, R. S.]—Medical department.

TULANE UNIVERSITY.*

Amendment to the Constitution.

SEC. 232. [Board of Administrators.]—The board of administrators of the University of Louisiana shall hereafter, instead of the board appointed as provided by section thirteen hundred and fifty-one (1351) of the Revised Statutes, consist of the seventeen administrators of the "Tulane Education Fund," with power, perpetually, to fill any vacancy in their number; provided, that the said board shall, on the passage of this statute, recognize by formal notarial act the Governor of the State, the Superintendent of Public Education, and the Mayor of the city of New Orleans, as ex-officio members of said board.

SEC. 233. [Rights, Powers, Franchises and Privileges of the Board.]—The board of administrators of the Tulane Education Fund, as administrators of the University of Louisiana shall have all the rights, powers, privileges, franchises, and immunities, now vested in the board of administrators of the University

---

*TULANE UNIVÉRSITY.—The University is not introduced into this compilation in the sense of a completely free school, yet the general benefits extended by its scholarship system, its agreement with the State and its relation to the ' University of Louisiana" place it in the catalogue of public institutions

The school was founded upon an endowment of the late Paul Tulane, and was established by Act No. 43 of 1884, which was ratified by a constitutional amendment April 17th, 1888. The following preamble, quoted from the above act, will explain the conditions upon which the "University of Louisiana" was changed into the Tulane University:

"*Whereas*, Paul Tulane, formerly a resident of this State, and now of Princeton, New Jersey, with the beneficent purpose of fostering higher education in this State di , in May, 1882, express to certain citizens of this State his intention to donate for such purposes valuable real estate to him belonging, situated in the city of New Or'eans; and

' *Whereas* The citizens to whom the intentions of Paul Tulane Esq., were expressed, did, by act, before Chas. G. Andry, a notary public in the city of New Orleans, organize themselv s into a corporation under the name of the 'Administrators of the Tulane Education Fund,' with the objects and purposes specified in said act of incorporation; and,

"*Whereas*, Since the formation of said corporation, Paul Tulane, Esq., in the execution of his previously expressed intentions, has donated to said administrators of the 'Tulane Education Fund' nearly one million dollars, the revenues whereof are to be used for the promotion and encouragement of intellectual, moral and industrial education, and has expressed his intention to largely increase said donation should this act be adopted ; and,

"*Whereas*, The said board of administrators of the Tulane Education Fund,' in order to make their work fruitful in results, have expressed their desire to take charge of the University of Louisiana, its ten years' of New Orleans, and to devote the revenues of the property now owned, or hereafter to be owned, by said board, to its expansion and development; and upon the adoption of a constitutional amendment to that end, to apply all the revenues of property now owned, or hereafter to be acquired by them to the creation and development in the city of New Orleans of a great University, whereby the blessings of higher education, intellectual, moral and industrial, may be given to the youth of this State ; and,

' *Whereas*, Under the terms of this action, as proposed by said board, the property of said board and the revenues thereof, will not be used for purposes of private or corporate income or profit, but will be exclusively dedicated to school purposes, and t) the service f the State in maintaining and developing the University of Louisiana, an institution recognized in the Constitution, therefore entitling the property of said board to exemption from all taxation both State, parochial and municipal ; therefore,

"*Be it enacted,*" eet.*

of Louisiana by existing laws. They shall further have full direction, control, and administration of the University of Louisiana, now established in the city of New Orleans, in all its departments, as also of all the property belonging to the State of Louisiana, and now dedicated to or used by the University of Louisiana, as well as all property controlled or used by the said University of Louisiana, and for the purposes thereof, and the board of administrators of the University of Louisiana are hereby empowered and directed to turn over to the board of administrators of the " Tulane Education Fund" all the property, rights, books, papers and archives now under their administration or control; provided, that if the custody of the State library should be transferred to the Tulane University of Louisiana, as herein established by the consolidation of the University of Louisiana at New Orleans with the board of administrators of the "Tulane Education Fund," as herein provided for, through the University of Louisiana, at New Orleans, as it now exists, or otherwise, it shall be on the express condition and agreement that the State of Louisiana may resume the custody and control of said State library, whenever it may be deemed advisable; and provided further, that after the establishment of the "Tulane University of Louisiana," as herein provided for, and after the transfer of the custody of the State library thereto, as aforesaid, if the custody thereof shall be transferred to the "Tulane University of Louisiana," as herein established, then and in that event, the State of Louisiana shall be relieved of and released from all obligations to pay the salary or the compensation of the State librarian or his assistants, as is now or may hereafter be fixed by law, during the period said State library may remain in the custody of the said "Tulane University of Louisiana;" but that during said period the salary or compensation of said State librarian shall be paid by the "Tulane University of Louisiana." An inventory shall be made of all the property, movable and immovable, belonging to the University of Louisiana, and transferred by this act to the control and administration of the administrators of the " Tulane Education Fund," by two appraisers to

be appointed for that purpose by the Governor of the State and
sworn, which appraisement shall be filed in the office of the Secretary of State, as evidencing the description and appraised value
of the property so transferred, and also in order that the liability
of the said administrators of the "Tulane Education Fund" may
not be extended beyond a return of the property so transferred,
in any contingency; provided further, that the property, so transferred, may not be sold or disposed of except under legislative
sanction; provided further, that if the "Tulane University of Louisiana" as herein established, should cease to use the property,
and exercise the privileges, franchises and immunities, now under
the control and administration of, and enjoyed by the University
of Louisiana, as now constituted and transferred by this act, for
the exclusive purposes intended by this act, then and in that
event the State of Louisiana shall have the right to resume the
custody, control, and administration of said. property, and the
exercise of said privileges, franchises and immunities.

SEC. 234. [Power to Own Property, Real and Personal.]—
The said board of administrators of the "Tulane Education
Fund"—shall perpetually as administrators of the University of
Louisiana as above provided, have full and complete control of
all the property and rights, and now vested in the University of
Louisiana. The said board shall have the powers above provided in addition to those conferred by its charter, by act passed
before Chas. G. Andry, notary public, in the city of New Orleans,
on the 29th day of May, A. D., 1882, including the power to hold
and own all real and personal property, now to said board
belonging, or hereafter to be by it acquired, during its corporate
existence, for the purposes and objects of its being, or the revenues whereof are to be solely applicable to such purposes.

SEC. 135. [Name: the Tulane University of Louisiana.]—In
honor of Paul Tulane and in recognition of his beneficent gifts
and of their dedication of their purposes expressed in this
act, the name of the University of Louisiana be, and the same is
hereby changed to that of the "Tulane University of Louisiana,"

under which name it shall possess all the powers, privileges, immunities and franchises, now vested in said University of Louisiana, as well as such powers as may flow from this act or may be vested in said board, under the term of this act, from the adoption of the constitutional amendment hereafter referred to. The purpose of this act, being, to invest the board of administrators of the "Tulane Education Fund" with all the rights now vested in the University of Louisiana; to give said board moreover complete control of said university in all its departments, and in every respect, with all powers necessary or incidental to the exercise of said control. To enable said board, besides the powers designated by this act, to have irrevocably upon the adoption of said constitutional amendment, full power with the rights hereby conferred to create and develop a great university in the city of New Orleans to be named as aforesaid; said university to be established by the said board of administrators of the "Tulane Education Fund," to be dedicated to the intellectual, moral and industrial education of the youth of the State, in accordance with the charter of said board of administrators of the Tulane Education Fund.

SEC. 236. [**Exemption from Taxation.**]—In consideration of the agreement of said board to develop and maintain the University of Louisiana, and thereby dedicate its revenues not to purposes of private or corporate income or profit, but to the public purposes of developing and maintaining the University of Louisiana, all the property of the said board, present and future, be and the same is hereby recognized as exempt from all taxation, State, parochial and municipal; this exemption to remain in force as long as the revenues of the said board are directed to the maintenance of the University of Louisiana, as aforesaid, or until said constitutional amendment be adopted. The adoption of said amendment shall operate such exemption in consideration of the said board expending their revenues as aforesaid, or creating, maintaining and developing a great university in the city of New Orleans; provided, that the property exempted from taxation

by this act shall not exceed in value five millions of dollars,
invested in real estate not otherwise exempted, which said value
shall be determined in the mode required by law for the assessment and valuation of property subject to taxation, it being the
true meaning and intent hereof, that all the property of the
Tulane University of Louisiana, of whatsoever character, shall
be exempted from taxation, State, parochial and municipal,
except the excess of real estate belonging thereto, over and
above the value of five million dollars, as above stated.

SEC 237. [Scholarships to be Granted.]—In consideration
of the vesting of the administration of the University of Louisiana · in the said administrators of the "Tulane Education
Fund," of the transfer of the rights, powers, privileges, franchises and immunities of the said university to said administrators and of the exemption from all taxation as herein above provided, the said administrators hereby agree and bind themselves,
with the revenues and income of the property heretofore given
them by Paul Tulane, Esq., as well as from the revenues of all
other property, real, personal, or mixed,· hereafter to be held,
owned or controlled by them, for the purposes of education, to
develop, foster, and maintain, to t e best of their ability and
judgment, the University of Louisiana, hereafter to be known as
the "Tulane University of Louisiana," and upon the adoption
of the constitutional amendment aforesaid, to perpetually use
the powers conferred by this act, and all power vested in them,
for the purpose of creating and maintaining in the city of New
Orleans a great university, devoted to the intellectual, moral
and industrial education and advancement of the youth of this
State, under the terms of the donation of Paul Tulane, and the
previous provisions of this act. The said board further agree
and bind themselves to waive all legal claim upon the State of
Louisiana for any appropriation, as provided in the Constitution
of this State, in favor of the University of Louisiana. Besides
the waiver of the claim, as aforesaid, as an additional consideration between the parties of this act, the said board agrees to give
continuously, in the academic department, free tuition to one

student from each senatorial and from each representative district or parish, to be nominated by its member in the General Assembly from among the *bona fide* citizens and residents of his district or parish, who shall comply with the requirements for admission established by said board. The meaning of this provision being that each member of the General Assembly, whether senator or representative, shall have the right of appointing one student, in accordance with the foregoing provisions. The free tuition herein provided for shall continue until each student has graduated from the academic department, unless his scholarship has ceased from other causes. Whenever a scholarship becomes vacant, from any cause, the senator or representative who appointed the previous student, or his successor, shall, in the manner prescribed by this section, immediately name a successor.

SEC. 238. [Contract Between the State and the University.]— This act, in all its provisions be and the same is hereby declared to be a contract between the State of Louisiana and the administrators of the "Tulane Education Fund," irrevocably vesting the said administrators of the "Tulane Education Fund" with the powers, franchises, rights, immunities and exemptions herein enumerated and hereby granted, and irrevocably binding said administrators to develop, foster, and maintain as above provided, the University as aforesaid in the city of New Orleans, subject to and according with the terms of this act.*

Laws Transferred from the University of Louisiana to the Tulane University of Louisiana.

SEC. 239. [Corporate Powers of the Board of Administrators.]— The administrators and their successors shall be and forever remain a body politic and corporate and shall have perpetual succession, and shall be able in law to sue and be sued, implead and be impleaded, answer and be answered

---

*The two sections succeeding this section in the Act 43 of 1884, which are sections 8 and 9, are hereby omitted, as their provisions are only temporary. The first prescribed that the act, without doubting the validity of the law, was to be submitted to the people for constitutional ratification; and the second made the act effective pending the constitutional election. Sections 10, 11 and 12 providing for election and containing repealing clauses are also omitted.

unto, defend and be defended in all courts and places whatsoever; and may have a common seal, and may change and alter
the same at their pleasure; and shall also be able in law to take
by purchase, gift, grant, devise and donation, *inter viros* and
mortis causa, made by individuals and corporations, within this
State or elsewhere, and to hold any real or personal estate whatever. They and their successors shall have power to grant, bar-
gain, sell, lease, demise or otherwise dispose of (except by mortgage) all or any part of the real or personal estate, as to them
shall seem best for the interests of the University, excepting the
buildings of the University, the library, apparatus and scientific
collections, which shall only be conveyed after the consent of
the Legislature is first obtained. No mortgage shall ever be
given on any of the property of the University, unless specially
authorized by law for any specific purpose.

SEC. 240. [**Departments of the University.**]—The University
shall be composed of the following departments or faculties, to-
wit: Law, Medicine, the Natural Sciences, Letters and College
proper, or Academical department; all of which, as the resources
of the University increase, shall be completed and the administrators, excepting the Medical department, which shall be composed of and formed by the Medical College of Louisiana, as at
present organized and established by law; which said department, as hereafter provided for, shall be engrafted on the University, and be conducted as hereafter directed.

SEC. 241. [**Powers of the Board of Administrators.**]—The
administrators shall have the power to direct and prescribe the
course of study and the discipline to be observed in the University; to appoint by ballot, or otherwise, the president of the
University, who shall hold his office at the pleasure of the board
and perform the duties of a professor; to appoint professors,
tutors and ushers to assist in the government and instruction of
the students, and such other officers as they may deem necessary,
they being removable at the pleasure of the board. They shall
fix the salaries of the president, professors and tutors, in the

Academical department, and fill vacancies in the professorships. Vacancies in the Law or Medical department shall be filled from persons first recommended to the administrators by the faculty of the department in which a vacancy may happen. No professor, tutor, or other assistant officer shall be an administrator of the University.

SEC. 242. [By-Laws and Regulations.]—They shall have power to make all ordinances and by-laws which to them shall seem expedient for carrying into effect the design contemplated by the establishment of this University, not inconsistent with the Constitution of the United States and of this State, nor with the provisions of their charter. They shall not make the religious tenets of any person a condition of the admission to any privilege or office in the University, nor shall any course of religious instruction be taught or allowed of a sectarian character and tendency.

SEC. 243. [Literary Honors and Degrees.]—They shall have the right of conferring under their common seal, on any person whom they may think worthy thereof, all literary honors and degrees known and usually granted by any university or college in the United States or elsewhere. The degree of Bachelor of Law, and Doctor of Medicine, granted by them, shall authorize the person on whom it is conferred to practice law, physic and surgery in this State.

SEC. 244. [Transfer of Property.]—All of the real and personal estate whatsoever belonging to the Medical College of Louisiana, is hereby transferred to and vested in the University of Louisiana; provided, the administrators of the University appropriate the sum which the real and personal estate of the Medical College cost to the purchase of philosophical and chemical apparatus for the use of the college, and the Medical College, as it is now organized, is herein and hereby incorporated with and made a part of the University of Louisiana, and shall constitute the only medical department of the University. The professors now filling the chairs in that school shall constitute the medical faculty of the department of medicine of the University, and fill the same chairs in the University now filled by them in the Medical School of Louisiana, and hereafter be under the government of the board of administrators of the University. The requisites for admission, the examination of candidates for their degrees in the medical and law departments, the management of pecuniary concerns, the salaries of the professors, the tuition and the terms of admission, shall be under the exclusive control of the faculty of the departments respectively.

SEC. 245. [Department of Law.]—The department of law shall consist of three or more professors, who shall be required to give a full course of lectures on international, constitutional, maritime, commercial and municipal or civil law, and instruction in the practice thereof.

SEC. 246. [Access of the Medical Department to the Charity Hospital.]—The medical department of the University shall at all times have free access to the Charity Hospital of New Orleans, for the purpose of affording their students practical illustrations of the subjects they teach.

INDEX.

AGRICULTURAL AND MECHANICAL COLLEGE, STATE UNIVERSITY AND,

    Constitutional provisions 7-9

    Legislative enactments 71

BLIND, INSTITUTE FOR THE 85

CITY SCHOOLS.

    School board 56

    Services of directors without compensation, superintendent......... 60

    Taxes prior to 1880, judgments, board of liquidation............. 61

    Treasurer 62

    Expenses, report of the board................................... 63

    Proper evidences of claims...................................... 64

COLORED UNIVERSITY.

    Constitutional clause... 7

    Southern University... 89

CONSTITUTIONAL PROVISIONS 4

DEAF AND DUMB, INSTITUTION FOR THE 87

DEBT.

    Evidences of debt non-negotiable 13

    Limit of contract obligations 15

DECISIONS AND APPEALS.

    Appeal of removed superintendent 12

    Decisions by the State Superintendent 22

DONATIONS.. 50

ENUMERATION OF EDUCABLE YOUTH.

    Parish superintendent's duty in relation thereto 24

    Assessor's duty... 25

EXAMINATIONS.

    Competitive 33

    Fee, duties of examiners 34

    Certificate, requirements 35

    Exception in regard to certain graduates........................ 26

EXEMPTION.
Schools from taxation 4
Officers from jury duty 18

EXPROPRIATIONS OF LAND...................................... 16

FRENCH LANGUAGE.
Constitutional provisions... 6
Legislative enactment............................. 53

FUNDS, SCHOOL.
Sectarian schools cannot receive 6
Of what they shall consist... 6
Free school, seminary, agricultural and mechanical 8
Transfer of, disbursement.. 27
Apportionment of.. 38

HYGIENE AND TEMPERANCE.
Shall be taught in the public schools.............................. 53

INDUSTRIAL COLLEGE, STATE.
Establishment and rules 69

INSTITUTES.
Attendance obligatory, penalty for superintendent's absence, parish
    institutes... 29
Members, managers, fund.. 30
Orleans excepted, reports, State institutes, conductor .... 31.
Assistant lecturers, notification to teachers...................... 32
Penalty for teacher's absence, leave of absence from schools, com-
    pensation, certificate, report................................ 33

LOUISIANA STATE UNIVERSITY 71

LAND FOR SCHOOL HOUSE SITES.
Expropriations 16
Sale by the Land Register 17

NORMAL SCHOOLS.
State Normal School.. 66

OATH OF OFFICE 12

PARISH OFFICERS.
Terms of office, removal... 12

PARISH SUPERINTENDENT.
Qualifications, salary, visits 23
Additional Compensation, teachers, enumeration of youth 24
Annual report, custody of papers.................................. 25
Oaths he may administer, office days 26
Penalty for absence from institute 29

REVENUE.

Apportionment of current school fund............................ 38
Police jury and municipal tax, bonds and fines 39
Special tax.......... 40
Poll tax.. 40
Sale of sixteenth section lands, election 43
. Survey, order of the Auditor.................................... 44
Unhabitable lands, sale... 45
Treasurer's commission, lease, proceeds 46
Annulling sales, collection of notes 47
Attorney's compensation.. 48
Capital due the several townships, trespass 49
Donations: authorized, conditions, trustees.................... 50
Trustees, fidei commissæ, of town charters 51
Prescription of debts 52

SCHOOL BOARD, PARISH.

Body corporate... 12
Evidence of debt non-negotiable, exempt from furnishing bonds in
    suits, attorney, duties and authority......................... 13
Debts, duties of president and secretary, reports 15
Expropriation of land for school house sites 16
School districts.. 18

SCHOOLS.

Graded and high schools.. 52
Branches to be taught, hygiene and temperance 53
Text books, sectarian schools, days of rest 54
    (See also CITY SCHOOLS.)

SIXTEENTH SECTIONS (See REVENUE).

STATE BOARD OF EDUCATION

Of whom composed 10
Time of meeting, may require reports, duties and powers 11

STATE INSTITUTIONS.

State Normal School.. 66
State Industrial College at Ruston 69
Louisiana State University and Agricultural and Mechanical College 71
Institute for the Blind... 85
Institute for the Deaf and Dumb................................ 87
Southern University (for Colored Persons) 89
Tulane University of Louisiana 92

STATE SUPERINTENDENT OF PUBLIC EDUCATION.

Office, salary, duties, expenses 20

Biennial report, suggestions for Deaf and Dumb Institute 21

Copies of records admissible in evidence, reports 22

Decisions and appeals.. 22

SUITS.

Exemption from furnishing bond, school board, attorney 13

TAX (See REVENUE).

TEACHERS.

Parish and State Teachers' Institutes 29

Examination and certificates of proficiency.................. 33

Accountability of pupils to teachers.............................. 36

TEXT BOOKS.

State Board of Education to adopt 11

Hygiene and Temperance 54

WOMEN ELIGIBLE TO SCHOOL OFFICES.

Constitutional clause 8

Same declared operative by legislative enactment 12

SYLLABI OF IMPORTANT SCHOOL DECISIONS

OF THE

SUPREME COURT.

CERTIFICATES OF INDEBTEDNESS.

The board of directors for the Public Schools of New Orleans have the control of school funds placed to their charge for the maintenance of the schools. It devolves upon this board to compel corporations to comply with their ordinances levying taxes for the schools, if they fail to comply with their obligation in this respect.

The board of directors have authority to stand in judgment; to institute or defend suits. The creditor of the school board has no right of action against the city of New Orleans to compel the city to recognize the validity of his claim.

School certificates of indebtedness issued by the board of directors of the Public Schools for the years 1874, 1875 and 1876, are not debts of the city of New Orleans, and actions for the purpose of having them recognized as valid claims can be maintained against the School Board, as it is authorized to pass on the validity of the evidence of indebtedness of every one who alleges that he is a creditor.

The city of New Orleans turns over amounts collected for schools to the treasurer of the School Board. This officer notes the taxes of different years and applies the amount to the payment of certificates from the taxes of these years from which the creditors are entitled to payment.—*Fisher et al. vs. School Directors*, 184, 44 *Ann.*

DEBTS OF DEFUNCT INSTITUTIONS.

The president of the board of supervisors of the Louisiana State University and Agricultural and Mechanical College cannot be compelled to warrant on any fund to pay a debt of either of the two former corporations, known respectively as "the Louisiana State University" and "the Agricultural and Mechanical College."—31 *Ann.*, 711, *State ex rel. Schorten, Agent, vs. President Board of Supervisors.*

A mere stated account between the superintendent of the Louisiana State University and Agricultural and Mechanical College, and one of the professors employed in that institution, signed by the superintendent, is not such conclusive proof of the amount due the professor as would enable the latter to mandamus the president of the board of supervisors of the institution to warrant for the amount, even if the president was authorized to draw such a warrant.—*Ib.*

EX CONTRACTU OBLIGATION.

The obligation of the Treasurer of the School Board of Union parish to account for funds received by him, is *ex contractu* and fiduciary in its character, and is only barred by the prescription of ten years.—32 *Ann.*, 793, *Board of School Directors of Union Parish vs. J. E. Trimble.*

FREE SCHOOL BONDS.

The sale of bonds constituting a part of the "free school fund," made in virtue of Act No. 81 of 1872, was utterly null and void, and conferred no title on the purchaser, and no future assignee or the purchaser, who took the bonds in good faith, for value, and before their maturity, could acquire a title to them.

Bonds that are a part of the assets of the "free school fund" are consigned by law to the custody of the Secretary of State and Auditor of Public Accounts, and those officers have a right to claim their possession in whatever hands they may be found. And this right is not affected by the prescription of three years.—31 *Ann.*, 1 5, *Sun Mutual Insurance Company vs. Board of Liquidation, Secretary of State and Auditor, Intervenors.*

LIMITATION OF CONTRACT.

The teachers of the public schools of New Orleans cannot, under the law, be appointed for a longer term than one year.— 34 *Ann.*, 354, *F. A. Golden vs. Board of Public School Directors of New Orleans.*

RECOVERY OF FUNDS.

Where a mistake has been made by the State Treasurer in announcing to the State Superintendent of Public Education the amount of funds for apportionment among the educable children of the State, but before the apportionment could be cancelled the school directors of Orleans had received their quota under it, when the true sum has been ascertained and announced to the superintendent, and a revised apportionment is to be made, it is proper that the superintendent should take into account, when apportioning to Orleans, the sum already improperly paid to her under the mistake, and which payment has been made in consequence of that mistake.—36 *Ann.*, 241, *The State ex rel. Board of School Directors, etc., vs. E. H. Fay, Superintendent, etc.*

A school board organized according to law has a right to stand in court to claim from another school board likewise constituted, school funds which should have been paid to it by the State authorities and which were illegally paid out to the latter. A receipt therefor would exonerate the debtor board.

If the funds are not in kind in the possession of said board, but can be traced to property in which they have been invested by such board, the property itself can be recovered in place of the funds which it represents.

An action to recover under such circumstances is not barred by the prescription of five years or less.—36 *Ann.*, 806, *School Board vs. School Board.*

SALE OF WARRANTS.

Under the authority of the Board of School Directors of a parish, the treasurer of the board may make a valid sale of the warrants of the State which represent that portion of the inte. est on the free school fund due to said parish.—31 *Ann.*, 158, *Board of School Directors of Concordia Parish vs. Hernandez.*

SCHOOL LAND, TENDER, ETC.

The residents and alleged tax payers in a township in whom is vested the title of the sixteenth section for the maintenance of the schools, have the right to invoke an interposition of the court to annul the sale of this section.

Tender as a prerequisite to the suit cannot be required. The price was not received by the plaintiffs. No title passed to the adjudicatee of the property.

The amount should be returned by the authority by which it was received. In the meantime plaintiffs can prosecute their suit to have the sale annulled.

The general government donated the sixteenth sections to the townships and authorized their sale, with the consent of the inhabitants residing within their respective limits. The legis-- lative department of the State in compliance with the conditions of the grant, adopted laws requiring elections to be held to ascer- tain the will of the majority of their voters residing within the townships and providing certain prerequisites for the sale. An election not having been held in the township, the return of the election not being sustained at all, the adjudication made was null.

The sixteenth section offered for sale should bring its ap- praised value, which may not be less than $1.25 per acre.— 44 *Ann.*, 365, *Telle et al. vs. School Board et al.*

SURETYSHIP.

Where the sureties on a five-thousand-dollar bond are jointly sued for an amount aggregating two thousand dollars, this court will have jurisdiction, although the demand against each surety is less than $500.—31 *Ann.*, 297, *State ex rel. School Board, Parish of St. Tammany vs. Cousin et al.*

Where the plaintiff who sues the sureties on an official bond alleges the hopeless insolvency of the principal, the sureties will not deprive themselves of the right of discussion, to which they are entitled under the law, by pleading an exception that admits the truth of the averment of insolvency.—*Ib.*

When the principal and sureties on an official bond are sued together, the judgment is *res adjudicata* as to the sureties, and within the limit of the amounts for which they are held under the terms of their bond, they are bound to make good the entire judgment against the principal, including the penalty.—40 *Ann.*, 705, *Eastin & Breaux vs. Board of School Directors.*

TAXATION.

The word "*may*" found in Section 54 of Act No. 81 of 1888, does not mean *shall.* Traced back, through the last sentence of Article 339 of the Constitution to Act No. 23, Section 28 of 1877, which the framers of that instrument intended to continue in force in that respect, it simply means are *authorized.*

The Constitution merely directed that the Legislature "shall provide that every parish *may* levy a tax,". which means *is authorized or empowered.*

Any legislation seeming to impose upon police juries the *duty* or *obligation* of levying the tax would transcend the delegated authority and so be unconstitutional and barren in effect.

Police juries are therefore clothed by law with the discretionary or optional power of levying or not, as their wisdom may see fit and proper, the tax in question for school purposes.

In case of failure to collect the tax, no *mandamus* can issue to compel the levy.—40 *Ann.*, 755, *State ex rel. School Directors vs. Police Jury.*

TAXATION.

A municipal corporation, sued under an enactment deemed by it to be unconstitutional, the object of which is to compel it to increase an appropriation from its alimony, has a right to plead the unconstitutionality of the act and to have the contention determined by the courts.

It cannot be called upon to show cause why a relief sought against it should not be granted and when it appears, in response, be met with the objection, that it has no standing in court and cannot be *heard*.

In such case, the courts will not refuse to listen to the defence; but will inquire and pass upon its merits.

The supremacy of a legislature over a city is not so absolute that it cannot be restrained by the organic law. Limitations imposed by the Constitution upon its powers cannot be overleaped.

The system of free schools in Louisiana is a State institution, for the establishment, maintenance and support of which the State is required to provide by taxation, or otherwise.

As a rule, the taxing powers may be exercised by the General Assembly for State purposes only, and by parish and municipal corporations, under authority granted them by the Legislature, for parish and municipal purposes alone; but, under express sanction of the Constitution, the General Assembly "may" authorize parishes to levy a tax for the public schools therein, not exceeding the State tax and, with other parish taxes, not exceeding the limits of parish taxation, fixed by the Constitution.

The Legislature cannot force a parish to levy a tax for school purposes. It may *authorize* it to do so, and when it has done so, and the parish undertakes to raise it, the constitutional limits must be observed.

To be valid, the levy of such a tax must find its authority in the organic law. The legislature has therefore no authority to *compel* the city of New Orleans, which is the parish of Orleans, to make an appropriation to stand in place of the amount which a school tax, if specially levied, would have realized.

The Legislature cannot transgress its powers, or invade those which are secured by the Constitution to the city of New Orleans. It can not do indirectly that which it is incompetent to do directly.

Although the first part of Section 71 of Act 81 of 1888, may be constitutional, the *provisos* which follow it and which require the city of New Orleans to appropriate no less than $250,000, for school purposes, are unconstitutional. They are, therefore, deemed unwritten and not binding on the city.—42, *Ann.*, 92, *State ex rel. School Board vs. City of New Orleans.*

THE STATE BOARD OF EDUCATION.

RESOLUTION

Passed by the State Board of Education on the 19th
day of October, 1894.

Resolved, That the Secretary of this board is hereby directed
to prepare a Compilation of School Laws, and to codify all enactments now in effect in such manner as to serve the convenience
of school officers as a book of legal reference, and he is authorized to add such annotations and appendices as he may deem
proper in interpreting the law.

8

THE STATE BOARD OF EDUCATION.

RULE I.—The elementary schools in cities and towns shall contain at least six grades, viz :—first, second, third (and possibly fourth), primary and first and second Grammar Departments; but such changes may be made by the local board as the condition of the locality may require.

RULE II.—In the primary departments there shall be taught: spelling, reading, phonetics, writing, geography, arithmetic and object lessons.

In the Grammar Departments, thorough instruction shall be given if the derivation of words, dictation, reading, writing, arithmetic, grammar, geography, history, elocution, composition, declamation, the natural sciences, and when possible, vocal and instrumental music, also drawing. It is recommended that the French language be taught in those localities, where the French population predominates, *provided*, the expenses of the school are not increased.

RULE III.—The High School, or Central School, shall continue the instruction of such youths as can pursue such studies as will best prepare them for admission to the Normal Schools, or to the freshman class of Tulane University and the freshman class of the Louisiana State University and A. and M. College.

RULE IV.—The Normal Schools shall have for their object the professional training of young men and women as teachers for the common schools of the State, and to thereby improve the standard of the public schools.

SCHOOL SESSIONS.

RULE V.—The scholastic year shall be deemed to commence on the second Monday of September of each year.

RULE VI.—The daily sessions shall not be less than five hours.

EXAMINATIONS.

RULE VII.—A public examination shall be held at least once each year. All the classes in the High Schools and Normal Schools shall be examined in writing in each branch of study when it is completed.

VACATIONS AND HOLIDAYS.

RULE VIII.—The schools shalls be closed on Saturdays and Sundays, and on such other days as may be directed by the Parish Boards.

TEACHERS.

RULE IX.—Teachers shall be at their respective rooms at least fifteen minutes before the hour of opening each session, and shall, in their daily registers, to be kept by the Principal, record the names and the time of arrival of each teacher; and any teacher not complying, shall be reported to the local superintendent, for such action as he may see proper under the laws, rules and regulations. The teachers shall remain on the school grounds, or in the premises, and exercise supervision over the pupils during each recess or intermission.

RULE X.—The jurisdiction and authority of the teacher over the pupils shall not be limited to the school house or enclosures nor to the actual session of the school. Generally in matters connected with the schools and the manners and morals of the scholars, his authority, with that of the parent, commences when pupils leave the parental roof and control, to go to school, and shall continue until their return from school. The teacher, however, shall not be responsible for the misconduct of pupils on the way to and from school, though he shall have the right to punish for misconduct when brought to his knowledge.

RULE XI.—The teachers shall bestow equal and impartial attention on all their pupils.

RULE XII.—It shall be their duty to practice such discipline in their schools as would be exercised by a kind and judicious parent in his family, always firm and vigilant but prudent. They shall endeavor on all proper occasions, to impress upon the minds of their pupils the principles of morality and virtue; a sacred regard for truth, reverence for the Creator, respect for one another, rectitude, industry and frugality. But no teacher shall exercise any sectarian or political influence in the school. They shall see that all pupils under their charge distinctly understand all rules relating to pupils, and they shall teach them the rules of health—hygiene and the bad effects of narcotics, as required by Act No. 40 of the General Assembly of 1888.

RULE XIII.—Any teacher who may be absent from school on account of sickness or other necessity must cause immediate notice to be given to the local superintendent. Teachers absent three consecutive days without cause may be considered as having abandoned their positions.

RULE XIV.—No teacher shall resign without giving two weeks notice to the local superintendent, else he may be made to forfeit one half month's pay.

RULE XV.—Teachers shall not hold any position of higher grade than the one corresponding to their certificates, nor shall the salary be larger than that allowed to the grade in which they teach.

RULE XVI.—All teachers shall attend the State and Parish Institutes, when notified by the superintendent.

PRINCIPAL TEACHERS.

RULE XVII.—The principal teachers shall keep a register, in which they shall record the name, age, birth place, residence, the names of the parents or guardians of each pupil entering the public schools, also the occupation of the parent or guardian.

RULE XVIII.—The principals shall be required within one week after the commencement of each term, to have the programme of their daily exercises posted in the school room, in a conspicuous place, and shall transmit a copy to the local super-intendent and one to the State superintendent.

RULE XIX.—They shall keep a daily record of all pupils admitted; those present. those absent or tardy.. They shall, at the end of each month, report the condition of their respective schools to the local superintendent, and file in his office, a copy of their respective registers, and, at the close of the school year, shall forward a certified copy of said register to the State Board of Educat on; they shall also keep records and make reports as required by Act No. 81, of the year 1888.

RULE XX.—The principal shall have supervisory control of the grounds, buildings and appliances, also, furniture and other common school property, and shall be held responsible for any want of neatness or cleanliness of the premises.

Whenever repairs are needed, the president of the school board should be notified by him.

PUPILS' ADMISSION.

RULE XXI.—Children entering the public schools are required to furnish all the necessary text-books and stationery used in their classes. The pupils are to be admitted in the primary schools not younger than six years. A pupil can begin school only on the first day of each week, and is to be accompanied at the time of his admission, by one of his parents, or guardian, or by a friend who will see to the proper registry of his name and furnish any further needful information.

RULE XXII.—They must attend the school established in the local school district in which they reside, or such school as the local board may designate.

RULE XXIII.—All transfers within the schools, or from one school to another, rendered necessary for any cause, shall be made by authority of the local superintendent. Pupils wishing transfers, must produce certificates from their former teachers, stating their reasons and the class to which they belonged.

RULE XIV.—No pupil shall be admitted to school after 10 o'clock, or allowed to depart before the appointed hour, except in case of sickness, or for other cause in the judgment of the teacher.

RULE XXV.—No pupil shall be admitted to the High School, unless he has undergone a sufficient and satisfactory examination.

DIRECTIONS TO SCHOOL OFFICERS AND OTHERS CONNECTED WITH THE PUBLIC SCHOOLS.

RULE XXVI.—Officers connected with the department of public schools, and all the employees are earnestly requested, indeed directed, to exert every reasonable endeavor to the promotion of the schools. They should avoid all antagonism and unkind opposition, but should never fail whenever opportunity offers, to exercise their influence in behalf of a system that gives to many youths of our State, the opportunity of escaping from the benighted condition of the absolutely illiterate.

In all matters of revenue for the schools, they should always endeavor to create a healthy condition, thereby assisting in setting aside (without its being a burden to any one) a sufficient amount to maintain a school system as it should be.

By co-operative action the schools will become the pride of the State and reflect its excellence, and the contributors will be more than rewarded by the improved condition.

RULES FOR THE EXAMINATION OF TEACHERS.

I.—Teachers shall not be examined to teach nor be given a certificate unless they enjoy a good moral character.

The committee of examiners shall cause teachers to appear before them and be examined in the branches they are to teach.

II.—The examination, when two or more apply for the same position, shall be competitive; the questions shall be answered in writing in presence of the examiners, in all branches in which such an examination is practicable.

III.—The written answers shall be examined, the merit marks or figures noted, and the candidate receiving the largest aggregate shall be preferred, *provided*, he is found competent.

IV.—A record of examination shall be kept by the local superintendent and shall be subject to the inspection of any officer connected with the schools.

Public notice should always be given of the day the examination will be held.

The appointee may be given charge of a school on probation during a period not longer than one month, during which time permanent engagement may be made—else he should not be employed, but paid for the services rendered.

STATE OF LOUISIANA,
DEPARTMENT OF EDUCATION.

THE

PUBLIC SCHOOL LAWS

OF 1896 AND 1898.

With Rules Adopted by the State Board of Education.

SUPPLEMENT TO THIRD COMPILATION.

ISSUED BY

J. V. CALHOUN,

Superintendent of Public Education.

BATON ROUGE:

THE ADVOCATE, OFFICIAL JOURNAL OF THE STATE OF LOUISIANA.

1898.

STATE OF LOUISIANA,
DEPARTMENT OF EDUCATION.

THE

PUBLIC SCHOOL LAWS

OF 1896 AND 1898,

With Rules Adopted by the State Board of Education.

SUPPLEMENT TO THIRD COMPILATION.

ISSUED BY

J. V. CALHOUN,
Superintendent of Public Education.

BATON ROUGE:
THE ADVOCATE, OFFICIAL JOURNAL OF THE STATE OF LOUISIANA.
1898.

NOTE.

This book contains all educational acts of a general character passed in the legislative sessions of 1896 and 1898, Some acts of a local character, especially those relating to prohibition of the sale of spirituous liquors near certain schools, are not here included. They must be sought in the regular publications of acts, as they are too numerous to be incorporated in this circular.

J. V. CALHOUN,
State Superintendent of Public Education.

CONSTITUTIONAL PROVISIONS.

Art. 230. (Educational Institutions Exempt from Taxation.)—The following shall be exempt from taxation, and no other, viz: All public property, places of religious worship, or burial, all charitable institutions, all buildings and property used exclusively for public monuments or historical collections, colleges and other school purposes, the real and personal estate of any library, and that of any other library association used by or connected with such library, all books and philosophical apparatus, and all paintings and statuary of any company or association kept in a public hall; provided, the property so exempted be not leased for purposes of private or corporate profit and income. * * * * * *

Art. 231. (Poll-Tax of one Dollar.)—The General Assembly shall levy an annual poll tax of one dollar upon every male inhabitant in the State between the ages of twenty-one and sixty years, for the maintenance of the public schools in the parishes where collected.

Art. 232. (School Tax on a Vote of Property Tax-Payers.)—The State tax on property for all purposes whatever, including expenses of government, schools, levees and interest, shall not exceed, in any one year, six mills on the dollar of its assessed valuation, and, except as otherwise provided in this Constitution, no parish, municipal or public board tax for all purposes whatsoever, shall exceed in any one year ten mills on the dollar of valuation; provided, that for giving additional support to public schools, and for the purpose of erecting and constructing public buildings, public school houses, bridges, wharves, levees, sewerage work and other works of permanent public improvement, the title to which shall be in the public, any parish, municipal corporation, ward or school district may levy a special tax in excess of said limitation, whenever the rate of such increase and the number of years it is to be levied and the purpose or purposes for which the tax is intended, shall have been submitted to a vote of the property taxpayers of each parish, ward or school district entitled to vote under the election laws of the State, and a majority of the same in numbers and in value voting at such election shall have voted therefor.

Art. 248. (Free Schools; for Whom; Apportionment of Funds.)—There shall be free public schools for the white and colored races, seperately established by the General Assembly, throughout the State, for the education of all the children of the State between the ages of six and eighteen years; provided, that where kindergarten schools exist, children between the ages of four and six may be admitted into said schools. All funds raised by the State for the support of public schools, except the poll tax, shall be distributed to each parish in proportion to the number of children therein between the ages of six and eighteen years. The General Assembly, at its next session shall provide for the enumeration of educable children.

Art. 249. (State Superintendent.)—There shall be elected by the qualified electors of the State a Superintendent of Public Education, who shall hold his office for the term of four years, and until his successor is qualified. His duties shall be prescribed by law, and he shall receive an annual salary of two thousand dollars. The aggregate annual expenses of his office, including his salary, shall not exceed the sum of four thousand dollars.

Art. 250. (State Board of Education; Parish Boards and Officers.)—The General Assembly shall provide for the creation of a State Board and Parish Boards of Public Education. The Parish Boards shall elect a Parish Superintendent of Public Education for their respective parishes, whose qualifications shall be fixed by the Legislature, and who shall be ex-officio secretary of the Parish Board. The salary of the Parish Superintendent shall be provided for by the General Assembly, to be paid out of the public school funds accruing to the respective parishes.

Art. 251. (French May be Taught.)—The general exercises in the public schools shall be conducted in the English language; provided, that the French language may be taught in those parishes or localities where the French language predominates, if no additional expense is incurred thereby.

At. 252. (Application of the Poll Tax.)—The funds derived from the collection of the poll tax shall be applied exclusively to the maintenance of the public schools as organized under this Constitution, and shall be applied exclusively to the support of the public schools in the parish in which the same shall be collected, and shall be accounted for, and paid by the collecting officer directly to the treasurer of the local school board.

Art. 253. (Sectarian Schools Cannot Receive Public School Funds.)—No funds raised for the support of the public schools of the State shall be appropriated to or used for the support of any private or sectarian schools.

Art. 254. (School Funds—Of what they Shall Consist.)— The school funds of the State shall consist of: 1st. Not less than one and one quarter mills of the six mills tax levied and collected by the State. 2d. The proceeds of taxation for school purposes as provided by this Constitution. 3d. The interest on the proceeds of all public lands heretofore granted or to be granted by the United States for the support of the public schools, and the revenue derived from such lands as may remain unsold. 4th. Of lands and other property heretofore and hereafter bequeathed, granted, or donated to the State for school purposes. 5th. All funds and property, other than unimproved lands, bequeathed or granted to the State, not designated for any other purpose. 6th. The proceeds of vacant estates falling under the law to the State of Louisiana. 7th. The legislature may appropriate to the same fund the proceeds of public lands not designated or set apart for any other purpose, and shall provide that every parish shall levy a tax for the public schools therein, which shall not exceed the entire State tax; provided, that with such a tax the whole amount of parish taxes shall not exceed the limits of parish taxation fixed by this Constitution. The City of New Orleans shall make such appropriations for the support, maintenance and repair of the public schools of said city as it may deem proper, but not less than eight tenths of one mill for one year; and said schools shall continue to receive from the Board of Liquidation of the City Debt, the amounts to which they are now entitled under the Constitutional amendment, adopted in the year 1892.

Art. 255. (State University and A. and M. College.)— The Louisiana State University and Agricultural and Mechanical College, founded upon the land grants of the United States to endow a seminary of learning and a college for the benefit of agriculture and mechanic arts, now established and located in the City of Baton Rouge, is hereby recognized; and all revenues derived and to be derived from the seminary fund, the Agricultural and Mechanical College fund, and other funds or lands donated or to be donated by the United States to the State of Louisiana for the use of a seminary of learning or of a college for the benefit of agriculture or the mechanic arts, shall be appropriated exclusively to the maintenance and support of the said Louisiana State University and Agricultural and Mechanical College; and the General Assembly shall make such additional appropriations as may be necessary for its maintenance, support, and improvement, and for the establishment, in connection with said institution, of such additional scientific or literary departments as the public necessities and the well being of the people of Louisiana may require; provided, that the appropriations shall not exceed fifteen thousand dollars per annum for its maintenance and support.

The Tulane University of Louisiana, located in New Orleans, is hereby recognized as created and to be developed in accordance with the provisions of the legislative act No.

43, approved July 5th, 1884, and by approval of the electors, made part of the Constitution of the State.

Art. 256. (Other State Schools.) The Louisiana State Normal School, established and located at Natchitoches; the Industrial Institute and College of Louisiana, whose name is hereby changed to the Louisiana Industrial Institute, established and located at Ruston; and the Southern University, now established in the city of New Orleans, for the education of persons of color, are hereby recognized; and the General Assembly is directed to make such appropriations from time to time as may be necessary for the maintenance, support and improvement of these institutions; provided, that the appropriation for the maintenance and support of the Louisiana Industrial Institute shall not exceed fifteen thousand dollars per annum, and that for the Southern University shall not exceed ten thousand.

Art. 257. (Interest Due the Townships.)—The debt due by the State to the free school fund is hereby declared to be the sum of one million, one hundred and thirty thousand, eight hundred and sixty seven dollars and fifty-one cents in principal, and shall be kept on the books of the Auditor and Treasurer to the credit of the several townships entitled to the same; the said principal being the proceeds of the sales of lands heretofore granted by the United States for the use and support of free public schools, which amount shall be held by the State as a loan, and shall be and remain a perpetual fund, on which the State shall pay an annual interest of four per cent, and said interest shall be paid to the several townships of the State entitled to the same, in accordance with the Act of Congress, No. 68, approved Februrary 15th, 1843.

Art. 258. (Debt Due Seminary Fund.) The debt due by the State to the seminary fund is hereby declared to be one hundred and thirty-six thousand dollars, being the proceeds of the sale of lands heretofore granted by the United States to this State for the use of a seminary or learning, and said amount shall be kept to the credit of said fund on the books of the Auditor and Treasurer of the State as a perpetual loan, and the State shall pay an annual interest of four per cent on said amount.

Art. 259. (Debt Due A. and M. College.) The debt due by the State to the Agricultural and Mechanical College fund is hereby declared to be the sum of one hundred and eighty-two thousand three hundred and thirteen dollars and three cents, being the proceeds of the sale of lands and land scrip heretofore granted by the United States to this State for the use of a college for the benefit of agricultural and mechanical arts; the said amount shall be kept to the credit of said fund on the books of the Auditor and Treasurer of the State as a perpetual loan, and the State shall pay an annual interest of five per cent on said amount.

Art. 260. (How Interest shall be Paid.) The interest due on the free school fund, the seminary fund and the Agricultural and Mechanical College fund, shall be paid out of any tax that may be levied and collected for the payment of the interest on the State debt.

Art. 261. (School Books for Indigent Pupils.) All pupils in the primary grades in the public schools throughout the Parish of Orleans, unable to provide themselves with the requisite books, an affidavit to that effect having been made by one of the parents of such pupils, or if such parents be dead, then by the tutor or other person in charge of such pupils, shall be furnished with the necessary books, free of expense, to be paid out of the school fund of said parish; and the School Board of the Parish of Orleans is hereby directed to appropriate annually not less than two thousand dollars for the purpose named, provided such amount be needed.

STATE UNIVERSITY.

No. 75.]

AN ACT

To amend and re-enact Section 6 of Act 145 of the Acts of 1876, consolidating the Louisiana State University and the Agricultural and Mechanical College.

Be it enacted by the General Assembly of the State of Louisiana; That Section 6 of Act 145 of 1876, be amended and re-enacted so as to read as follows: That the Governor of the State shall be a member and ex-officio president of the Board of Supervisors and the State Superintendent of Public Education and the President of the Faculty of the University shall also be members ex-officio of said Board, and the twelve remaining members shall be appointed by the Governor, by and with the advice and consent of the Senate, provided, that at least six of the fifteen supervisors of the University shall have been students of the Louisiana State University or of the Louisiana State University and Agricultural and Mechanical College, and shall have taken degrees and be titled graduates of one of said institutions.

At least one member of said Board of Supervisors shall be appointed from the parish of East Baton Rouge. Whenever a vacancy occurs in said Board for any cause the same shall be filled for the unexpired term. The terms of office of the present members of the Board of Supervisors as now constituted under appointements heretofore made, shall in no manner be abridged, terminated or affected by the provisions of this act, but whenever a vacancy shall hereafter occur for any cause in the Board of Supervisors, the same shall be filled by the appointment of a titled graduate of one of said institutions until at least six titled graduates aforesaid shall be members of said Board of Supervisors, and said Board shall be thereafter so constituted and maintained.

S. P. HENRY,
Speaker of the House of Representatives.
R. H. SNYDER,
Lieutenant Governor and President of the Senate.
Approved July 9th, 1896.
MURPHY J. FOSTER,
Governor of the State of Louisiana.
A true copy:
JOHN T. MICHEL,
Secretary of State.

STATE BOARD OF EDUCATION.

No. 85.]

AN ACT

To amend and re-enact Section 1, 2, and 18 of Act No. 81 of 1888, entitled "An act in relation to free public schools, and to regulate public education in the State of Louisiana; to provide a revenue for the same, and impose certain penalties; to apply fines imposed by district courts, and amounts collected on bonds, to the payment of public education, and to provide for payment of unpaid balances due to the public school teachers of New Orleans, for the years eighteen hundred and eighty (1880), eighteen hundred and eighty-one (1881), eighteen hundred and eighty-two (1882), and eighteen and eighty-four (1884.)

Section 1. (State Board of Education.)—Be it enacted by the General Assembly of the State of Louisiana, that Section 1 of Act 81 of 1888, be amended and re-enacted so as to read as follows:

The Governor and the Superintendent of Public Education and the Attorney General, together with six citizens to be appointed by the Governor, one from each Congressional district of the State, shall be a body politic and corporate by the name and style of the State Board of Education for the State of Louisiana, with authority to sue and defend suits in all matters relating to the interests of the public schools.

The above specified six citizens shall receive as compensation for their services, in attending the meetings of the Board their actual traveling expenses and per diem for the number of days that the Board is in session, the same as members of the State Legislature, payable on their warrants, approved by the President or acting President of the Board.

The Board may appoint a Secretary, whose salary shall not exceed $300.00 (Three Hundred Dollars) a year, and shall be fixed by the Board, payable semi-annually on the warrant of the President of the Board.

Sec. 2. (Publication of Proceedings.)—Be it further enacted, etc., That Section 2 of Act 81, of 1888 shall be amended and re-enacted so as to read as follows:

The Governor shall be ex-officio President. The Board shall meet on or before the first Monday of December of each year, and at other times upon the call of the State Superintendent. All papers, documents, and records appertaining to the Board shall be filed by the Secretary in the office of the State Superintendent of Public Education. The State Superintendent may publish, if he sees fit, or at the request of the Board, the proceedings of the State Board of Education in the official journal of the State, or in an official pamphlet, as he sees fit.

The acts of the Board shall be attested by the President.

Sec. 3. (Ex-Officio Positions of State Superintendent.)—Be it further enacted, etc., That Section 18 of Act 81 of 1888 shall be amended and re-enacted so as to read as follows:

The State Superintendent of Public Education shall have general supervision of all Parish School Boards in the parishes, and of all Common, High, or Normal Schools of the State, and shall see that the school system of the State is carried into effect properly. He shall be ex-officio a member of the Board of Supervisors of the State University and Agricultural and Mechanical College, the State Normal School, the State Industrial School at Ruston, the Institute for the Deaf and Dumb, and the Institution for the Blind, and all other institutions of learning under the control of the State.

He shall visit all the parishes of the State, whenever practicable, at least once a year, and shall give due notice of the time of his visit to the Parish Superintendent, whose duty it shall be to meet and confer with the State Superintendent on all matters connected with the interests of the Common Schools of the parish. His expenses incurred in the discharge of this duty shall be paid out of the general fund, but shall not exceed the amount appropriated per annum for the purpose.

Sec. 4. Be it further enacted, etc., That all laws, or parts of laws in conflict with the foregoing be and the same are hereby repealed.

S. P. HENRY,
Speaker of the House of Representatives.
R. H. SNYDER,
Lieutenant Governor and President of the Senate.
Approved July 9th, 1896.
MURPHY J. FOSTER,
Governor of the State of Louisiana.
A true copy:
JOHN T. MICHEL,
Secretary of State.

STATE NORMAL SCHOOL.
No. 91.]
AN ACT
To amend and re-enact Section 9 of Act No. 73, of 1892.

Section 1. Be it enacted by the General Assembly of the State of Louisiana, That Section 9 of Act No. 73, of 1892, be amended and re-enacted so as to read as follows:

Sec. 9. (State Normal School Diplomas.)—The Board of Administrators of the State Normal School is hereby empowered to confer diplomas upon all graduates of said school. This diploma shall entitle the holder to a first grade teacher's certificate without examination, and shall be valid in any part of the State for four years from the date of graduation, after the expiration of which time it may be renewed every four years, for the same period, by said Board of Administrators upon satisfactory evidence of the ability, progress and moral character of the teacher making application for such renewal. Furthermore, the diploma of the State Normal School shall entitle its holder to such degree of preference in the selection of teachers for the Public Schools of the State as may be deemed wise and expedient by the State Board of Education.

Sec. 2. Be it further enacted, etc., That all laws, or parts of laws, in conflict with the provisions of this Act be and the same are hereby repealed.

S. P. HENRY,
Speaker of the House of Representatives.
R. H. SNYDER,
Lieutenant Governor and President of the Senate.
Approved July 9th, 1896.
MURPHY J. FOSTER,
Governor of the State of Louisiana.
A true copy:
JOHN T. MICHEL,
Secretary of State.

EXPROPRIATIONS.

No. 96.]

AN ACT

To amend and re-enact Section Fourteen Hundred and Seventy-nine (1479) of the Revised Statutes of the State of Louisiana as amended by Act 117 of 1886, and to provide for the expropriation of property for purposes of Charity Hospitals and of Public Schools.

Section 1. (Expropriation of Property for Public Schools.) —Be it enacted by the General Assembly of the State of Louisiana, that Section 1479 of the Revised Statutes of the State of Louisiana be amended and re-enacted so as to read as follows:

Whenever the State or any political corporation of the same, created for the purpose of exercising any portion of the government powers in the same, or the Board of Administrators of any Charity Hospital or any Board of Public School Directors thereof, or any corporation constituted under the laws of this State for the construction of a railroad, plank road, turn pike, road or canal for navigation or for the purpose of transmitting intelligence by magnetic telegraph, can-

not agree with the owner of any land which may be wanted
for its purchase, it shall be lawful for such State Corporation
or Board to apply, by petition, to the District Court in which
the same may be situated; or, if it extends into two Districts,
to the Judge of either District Court in which the owner re-
sides; and if the owner does not reside in either District, then
to either of the District Courts, describing the lands necessary
for the purpose, with a plan of the same and a statement of
the improvements thereon, if any, and the name of the owner
thereof, if known, at present in the State, with a prayer that
the land be adjudged to such State, corporation or board upon
payment to the owner of all such damages as he may sustain
in consequence of the expropriation of his land for such public works; all claims for land or damages to the owner caused
by its taking or expropriation for such public works shall be
barred by two (2) years prescription, which shall commence
to run from the date at which the land was actually occupied
and used for the construction of the works.

Sec. 2. Be it further enacted, etc., That all the existing
laws for the form and process of expropriation of property
shall be applicable to the said section as thus amended and re-
enacted.

S. P. HENRY,

Speaker of the House of Representatives.

R. H. SNYDER,

Lieutenant Governor and President of the Senate.

TEACHERS' INSTITUTES.

No. 111.]

AN ACT

Relative to State and Parish Teachers' Institutes, and amending and re-enacting Act No. 64 of 1894, entitled, "An Act
to provide for holding State Teachers' Institutes in the
several parishes."

Be it enacted by the General Assembly of the State of
Louisiana, that Act No. 64 of 1894 be amended and re-enacted
so as to read as follows:

Section. 1. (Institute: Time and Place, Notice.)—Be it enacted, etc., That as a means of improving and making more
efficient the Public Schools of the State of Louisiana, and
awakening a deeper public interest in said schools, the State
Superintendent of Public Education and the President of the
State Normal School shall cause to be held each year as many
State Teachers' Institutes or Summer Normal Schools of not
less than four consecutive weeks each, as the funds at their
disposal may warant, at such time and places as they, with the
advice of the respective Parish Superintendents of Public Edu-

cation, may determine. They shall give notice of the time and place elected for each State Institute at least thirty days before the beginning of said Institute.

Sec. 2. (Institute Conductor.)—Be it further enacted, etc., That the State Superintendent of Public Education and the President of the State Normal School shall select an experienced Institute Conductor, who shall have general charge of the State and Parish Institutes provided for in this Act, and whose salary for that service shall not exceed one thousand ($1000) dollars per annum, payable out of any funds donated by the Board of Trustees of the Peabody Education Fund or appropriated by the General Assembly of the State of Louisiana for Institute purposes.

Sec. 3. (Term of Conductor.)—Be it further enacted, etc., That said Institute Conductor shall be appointed for one year, and shall be ex-officio a member of the faculty of the State Normal School, performing therein such services and receiving such compensation therefor as the Board of Administrators of said institution may determine.

Sec. 4. (Assistants.)—Be it further enacted, etc., That said Institute Conductor shall be assisted in the work by members of the faculty of the State Normal School and by such other assistants as the State Superintendent of Public Education and the President of the State Normal School may select; provided, that members of the State Normal School faculty shall receive no compensation other than their actual traveling expenses for Institute work done during the session of said institutions; but for Institute work done during the vacation of said Normal School, they in common with the other assistants, shall receive such remuneration as the State Institute managers may deem sufficient, payable out of any funds derived from the Peabody fund or appropriated by State, parish or locality for Institute purposes.

Sec. 5. (Parish Institutes Mandatory.)—Be it further enacted, etc., That every Parish Superintendent be and is hereby not only empowered, but required, to hold an institute of one week every year for teachers of his parish, according to a programme made out by the State Institute Conductor, and approved by the State Superintendent of Public Education and the President of the State Normal School. Said Parish Institute shall be held at some convenient locality, and every teacher then employed in said parish, or who expects to be employed for the next session of the schools, shall be required to attend said institute. Public notice of the time and place of this institute shall be given at least thirty days before the opening thereof. The expenses of said Parish Institute shall be defrayed by the Parish School Board out of the examination fees of teachers, or any other funds at their disposal.

Sec. 6. (State Institute Managers.)—Be it further enacted, etc., That the State Superintendent of Public Education and the President of the State Normal School, with the State Institute Conductor, shall be known as the State Institute Managers, and shall prescribe the order and character of the Institute exercises and such other details as may be deemed necessary.

Sec. 7. (Notice to Teachers.)—Be it further enacted, etc., That the Parish Superintendent, with the advice of the State Institute Conductor, shall make all necessary arrangements for the State and parish teachers' institutes to be held in this parish, and shall do everything in his power to insure their success. He shall give to every public school teacher of his parish, required by law to attend the institute, at least fifteen days' written notice of the time and place of the meeting of the institute, and shall order all the public schools of his parish to be closed during the session of the institute.

Sec. 8. (Penalty for Non-Attendance.)—Be it further enacted, etc., That any public school teacher failing to attend the State or parish institute held in his parish, without an excuse satisfactory to the Board of School Directors thereof, shall immediately upon the demand of the Parish Superintendent, forfeit his certificate and lose his position.

Sec. 9. (Leave of Absence from Schools, etc.)—Be it further enacted, etc., That the School Superintendent of every parish in which no State Institute is to be held during theyear shall encourage and urge the public school teachers of his parish to attend the nearest State Institute, granting them leave of absence from their school duties; providing, that in all cases where the school session is actually in progress, or is to be begun during the time of holding either the State or the Parish Institute, whether the former be held in his own parish or not, the time thus consumed by the teacher in attendance upon the institute shall be extended to him after the institute shall have been held, and he shall be required to teach the full term for which he has contracted.

Sec. 10. (Certificates of Attendance.)—Be it further enacted, etc., That the State Institute Conductor or his assistant conductors shall issue certificates of attendance to every teacher present during the whole session of the State or parish teacher's institute, and the parish boards of school directors shall give preference, other things being equal, to the holders of said certificates, in the selection of teachers for the public schools.

Sec. 11. (Institute Reports.)—Be it enacted, etc., That the State Institute Conductor shall annually make an exhaustive report of the State Teachers' Institutes, and shall submit this report with a detailed account of all institute funds received and disbursed by him, to the President of the State Normal School, who shall transmit said report to the State Superintendent of Public Education for publication in his biennial report to the General Assembly.

Sec.12. Be it further enacted, etc., That all laws or parts of laws in conflict with the provisions of this Act be and the same are hereby repealed.

S. P. HENRY,
Speaker of the House of Representatives,
R. H. SNYDER,
Lieutenant Governor and President of the Senate.

Approved July 9, 1896.

MURPHY J. FOSTER,
Governor of the State of Louisiana.

A true copy:
JOHN T. MICHEL,
Secretary of State.

SCHOOL INDEMNITY LANDS.

Act No. 87.]

AN ACT

To amend and re-enact Act No. 152 of the Acts of 1890, to provide for the sale of school indemnity lands.

Section 1. Be it enacted by the General Assembly of the State of Louisiana, That all lands now owned by or which may hereafter inure to the State from the United States Government, as indemnity for school lands, shall be disposed of as hereinafter provided.

Section 2. Be it further enacted, etc., That the Register of the State Land office shall have advertised for the sale at public auction, for thirty clear days, a list of the lands to be sold; the publication to be made in a newspaper published in the parish where the land to be sold is situated, and no land to be sold need be advertised in any paper outside of the parish where the land to be sold is situated; provided that no improved lands shall be advertised under the foregoing provisions unless requested by the Board of School Directors of the parish in which the land is located.

Section 3. Be it further enacted, etc., That the land shall be sold at public auction at the office of the Register of the State Land office and shall be adjudicated to the last and highest bidder; provided in no case shall it be sold for less than two dollars and a half per acre.

Section 4. Be it further enacted, etc., That any land which fails to bring the price of two dollars and a half per acre when offered at auction shall thereafter be subject to private sale at two dollars and a half per acre.

Section 5. Be it further enacted, etc., That it shall be the duty of the Register to deposit in the State Treasury to the credit of the various school boards entitled to receive the same the proceeds of the sale of all indemnity school lands after paying the expense of advertising.

S. P. HENRY,
Speaker of the House of Representatives.
R. H. SNYDER,
Lieutenant Governor and President of the Senate,
Approved July 9th, 1898.
MURPHY J. FOSTER,
Governor of the State of Louisiana.
A true copy:
JOHN T. MICHEL,
Secretary of State.

PARISH SUPERINTENDENT.

Act No. 92.]

AN ACT

To amend and re-enact Section 25 of Act 81 of 1888, entitled, "An act in relation to free public schools and to regulate public education in the State of Louisiana; to provide a revenue for the same and to impose certain penalties and to apply fines imposed by the district court, and amounts collected on bonds, to the purpose of public education, and to provide for the payment of unpaid balances due to the public school teachers of New Orleans, for the years eighteen hundred and eighty (1880), eighteen hundred and eighty-one (1881), eighteen hundred and eighty-two (1882), and eighteen hundred and eighty-four (1884).

Section 1. Be it enacted by the General Assembly of the State of Louisiana, That Section 25 of Act 81 of 1888, be amended and re-enacted so as to read as follows: The parish board of school directors shall elect a parish superintendent, who shall be ex-officio secretary of the board, in each parish of the State, the parish of Orleans excepted, who shall be possessed of moral character and ability to manage the common school interests of the parish, and who shall be of age and a qualified elector. His salary shall be fixed by the parish school board, provided that in no case shall it be less than two hundred dollars ($200), nor more than twelve hundred dollars ($1200) per annum.

S. P. HENRY,
Speaker of the House of Representatives.
R. H. SNYDER,
Lieutenant Governor and President of the Senate.

Approved July 12th, 1898.

MURPHY J. FOSTER,
Governor of the State of Louisiana.

A true copy:
　　JOHN T. MICHEL,
　　　Secretary of State.

ENUMERATION OF YOUTH.

Act No. 129.]

AN ACT

To provide for the enumeration of the educable children of the State, and to fix the compensation therefor.

Section 1. Be it enacted by the General Assembly of the State of Louisiana, That the Assessors of all the parishes of the State, including the Board of Assessors of the Parish of Orleans, shall make an enumeration of all the educable children of the State before July 1st, 1899, and every four years thereafter.

Section 2. Be it further enacted, etc., That it shall be the duty of the Assessors and the Board of Assessors of the Parish of Orleans to make a correct enumeration by giving the names of the educable children, between the ages of six and eighteen years in the respective parishes by race, sex and ward. This list of educable children shall be made in triplicate form, and written in ink. One list shall be furnished to the Auditor of Public Accounts, one list to the State Board of Education, and one list to the Board of School Directors of the Parish in which the enumeration is made. It shall be the duty of the Assessors and the Board of Assessors of the parish of Orleans to swear to the correctness of said list or lists before a competent officer, who shall attach a certificate thereof on each list before filing them.

Section 3. Be it further enacted, etc., That the parish Boards of School Directors shall pay the Assessors four cents for the enumeration of each educable child in their respective parishes on the approval of the work of enumeration by the State Board of Education, which shall be signified to the parish Boards by the Secretary of State Board under seal. In the event the State Board of Education for any cause deems the enumeration made incorrect or improperly made out, it shall have the power and authority to order a new enumeration in the parishes where the inaccuracies are found, without extra compensation.

Section 4. Be it further enacted, etc., That it shall be the duty of the Auditor of Public Accounts to furnish blank forms ruled to set forth the required names of the educable children by wards, with the race, sex, and age of the children, to the Assessors and the Board of the parish of Orleans.

Section 5. Be it further enacted, etc.,That in case of wilful negligence and refusal to comply with the provisions of this Act, the Governor shall have the power and authority to remove any Assessor or member of the Board of Assessors from office for such refusal or negligence.

Section 6. Be it further enacted, etc., That all laws or parts of laws in conflict with the provisions of this act be and are hereby repealed.

S. P. HENRY,
Speaker of the House of Representatives.
R. H. SNYDER,
Lieutenant Governor and President of the Senate.
Approved July 13th, 1898.
MURPHY J. FOSTER,
Governor of the State of Louisiana.
A true copy:
JOHN T. MICHEL,
Secretary of State.

SPECIAL ELECTIONS. IMPROVEMENTS.

Act No. 131.]

AN ACT

To prescribe the manner in which special elections shall be held in any parish, municipality, ward, or school district of this State, for the purpose of levying special taxes for the support of public schools, and for the purpose of erect-ing and constructing public buildings, public school houses, bridges, wharves, levees, sewerage work and other works of permanent improvement, the title to which shall be in the public, in such parish, municipality, ward, or school district, and to carry into effect Article 233, of the Constitution of 1898.

Section 1. Be it enacted by the General Assembly of the State of Louisiana, That whenever one-third of the property tax-payers of any parish, municipality, ward, or school district in this State shall petition the Police Jury of such parish, or the municipal authorities of such municipality, to levy a special tax for the support of public schools, and for the purpose of erecting and constructing public buildings, public school-houses, bridges, wharves, levees, sewerage work and other works of permanent public improvement, the title to which shall be in the public, the said Police Jury or municipal authorities shall order a special election for that purpose, and submit to the property tax-payers of each parish, municipality, ward, or school district, the rate of taxation, the number of years it is to be levied and the purposes for which it is intended; provided, that said election be held under the general election laws of the State, and at the polling places at which the last preceding general election was held, and not sooner than thirty days after the official publication of the petition and ordinance ordering the election.

Section 2. Be it further enacted, etc., That the petition mentioned in Section 1, of this act shall be in writing, and shall designate the object and amount of the tax to be levied each year, and the number of years during which it shall be levied.

Section 3. Be it further enacted, etc., That if a majority in number and value of the property tax-payers of such parish, municipality, ward or school district voting at such election, shall vote in favor of such levy of said special tax, then the Police Jury, on behalf of such parish, ward, or school district, or the municipal authorities, authorities for and on behalf of such municipality shall immediately pass an ordinance levying such tax, and for such time as may have been specified in the petition, and shall designate the year in which such taxes shall be levied and collected.

Section 4. Be it further enacted, etc., That all tax-payers voting at said election shall be registered voters, except women tax-payers, who shall vote without registration. All tax-payers entitled to vote shall do so in person except women who shall vote either in person or by their agents, authorized in writing.

Section 5. Be it further enacted, etc., That the Police Jury of any parish, ward, or school district, or the municipal authorities of any municipality, shall, when the vote is in favor of the levy of such taxes, levy and collect annually, in addition to other taxes, a tax upon all taxable property within such parish, municipality, ward, or school district, sufficient to pay the amount specified to be paid in such petition, and such police jury and authorities shall have the same right to enforce and collect any special tax that may be authorized by such election, as is or may be conferred by law upon them for the collection of other taxes, which taxes so collected shall be used for the purpose named in said petition, and in the case of a tax being named for the support of a public school, or for the purpose of erecting a public school-house, the same shall from time to time, as the same is collected, be paid to the board of school directors of the parish in which said tax is levied, and be used for the purpose stated in said petition.

S. P. HENRY,

Speaker of the House of Representatives.

R. H. SNYDER,

Lieutenant Governor and President of the Senate.

Approved July 13th, 1898.

MURPHY J. FOSTER,

Governor of the State of Louisiana.

A true copy:

JOHN T. MICHEL,

Secretary of State.

TRANSFER OF FUNDS.

Act No. 104.]

CONCURRENT RESOLUTION.

Whereas, Art. 257, of the Constitution, fixes the debt due by the State to the Free School Fund at one million, one hundred and thirty thousand, eight hundred and sixty-seven dollars and fifty-one cents ($1,130,867.51), and

Whereas, an annual interest of four per cent. is required by said article to be paid on said sum, and

Whereas, Art. 260 requires the interest on said amount to be paid out of any tax that may be levied and collected for the payment of the interest on the State debt, and

Whereas, the sum of forty-five thousand, two hundred and thirty-four dollars and seventy cents ($45,234.70) is appropriated annually for the purpose of paying the interest above mentioned, and

Whereas, according to the amounts credited on the township ledger, only the sum of thirty-eight thousand, one hundred and eighteen dollars and three cents ($38,118.03) is annually used in paying said interest.

Therefore, Be it resolved by the House of Representatives of the State of Louisiana, the Senate concurring, That the difference between the amount appropriated and the amount actually used in paying the interest on the several townships be and the same is hereby transferred annually from the Interest Tax Fund to the Current School Fund, and that the Auditor of Public Accounts be and he is hereby directed to carry out the provisions of this resolution.

S. P. HENRY,
Speaker of the House of Representatives.
ALBERT ESTOPINAL,
President pro tem. of the Senate.

Approved July 11th, 1898.
MURPHY J. FOSTER,
Governor of the State of Louisiana.

A true copy:
JOHN T. MICHEL,
Secretary of State.

SOUTHERN LOUISIANA INDUSTRIAL INSTITUTE.

Act No. 162.]

AN ACT

To create and establish a State Industrial Institute for the Education of white children of the State of Louisiana in the arts and sciences.

Section 1. Be it enacted by the General Assembly of the State of Louisiana, That, a State Industrial Institute is hereby established for the education of the white children of the State of Louisiana, in the arts and sciences.

Said Institute shall be known as the "Southwestern Louisiana Industrial Institute," and shall be located in that parish of the 13th Senatorial District which will offer the best inducement therefor to the Board of Trustees, said location to be made by the Board to be appointed under this act, provided that the parish selected for the location of said Institution shall donate not less than twenty-five acres of land and Five Thousand Dollars to said Institution, and the same shall be organized as hereinafter provided; provided further that in case two or more of said parishes offer the same inducements then the Board of Trustees shall select, by a majority vote, the most suitable location and make report thereof to the

General Assembly of the State of Louisiana, at its next session, together with such recommendations as may be conducive to the best interests of said institution.

Sec. 2. Be it further enacted, etc., That the Governor of the State shall nominate and appoint, by and with the advice and consent of the Senate, one person from each Congressional District of this State, and two from the State at large, to be trustees, and to serve as herein provided. Immediately after they shall be assembled, in consequence of their first appointmnt, they shall be divided by lot into two equal classes, so that the term of three of those appointed from the Congressional Districts, and one appointed from the State at large shall expire in two years, and the term of the other half shall expire in four years from the date of their appointment; so that one half may be chosen every two years. Vacancies shall be filled as in case of other offices in this State. The Governor of the State and State Superintendent of Public Education shall be ex-officio members of said Board of Trustees, and the Governor shall, when present, act as president of the Board, but the Board shall elect one of their number Vice-President. Five of the Trustees shall constitute a quorum for the transaction of business.

Sec. 3. Be it further enacted, etc., That the Board of Trustees of said Institute be and the same are hereby declared a body politic and corporate; shall be domiciled at the parish seat of the parish where the Institution will be located; shall sue and be sued, contract and be contracted with; may hold, purchase, sell and convey property, whether movable or immovable, which may be necessary or beneficial in carrying out the purposes of this act. Said Board of Trustees may provide under proper regulations and rules for conferring degrees and awarding diplomas and granting certificates, as rewards and honors for learning and skill, to the pupils of said Institute.

Sec. 4. Be it further enacted, etc., That said Board of Trustees shall fix the time or times for regular meetings, and may be convened at any time the Governor as ex-officio President may deem it expedient to do so, in order to transact business connected with said Institute.

The President of the Faculty and teachers shall be Secretary of the Board of Trustees, and he shall keep in a well bound book, a record of the proceedings had by said Board, and his compensation for this service shall be fixed by the Board; provided that said Board may elect a suitable person as Secretary pro tem. to act until the Institute be put in operation.

Sec. 5. Be it further enacted, etc., that the said Board of

Trustees shall possess all the power necessary and proper for the accomplishment of the trust reposed in them, viz.: The establishment of a first-class Industrial Institute for the education of the white children of Louisiana in the arts and sciences, at which such children may acquire a thorough academic and literary education, together with a knowledge of kindergarten instruction, of telegraphy, stenography and photography, of drawing, painting, designing and engraving in their industrial applications; also a knowledge of fancy, practical and general needle-work; also a knowledge of bookkeeping and agricultural and mechanical art together with such other practical industries as, from time to time, may be suggested to them by experience, or such as will tend to promote the general object of said institute, to-wit: Fitting and preparing such children, male and female, for practical industries of life.

Sec. 6. Be it further enacted, etc., That the Board of Trustees shall select and appoint a president and the professors of said institute, and such other officers as they may deem necessary to put and maintain the same in successful operation, and shall make such rules and regulations for the government of said officers as they may deem advisable; they shall prescribe such a course of discipline as may be necessary to enforce the faithful discharge of the duties of all officers, professors and students. They shall prescribe the course or courses of instruction so as to secure thorough education and the best possible instruction in all of said industrial studies, and they shall adopt all such by-laws and regulations as they may deem necessary to carry out all the purposes and objects of said Institution.

Sec. 7. Be it further enacted, etc., That all the property acquired in any way by said Board of Trustees shall really be the property of and belong to the State of Louisiana, but shall be held, controlled and managed by said Board of Trustees for the benefit of said Industrial Institute.

Sec. 8. Be it further enacted, etc., That said Board of Trustees shall be convened as soon as practicable.

S. P. HENRY,
Speaker of the House of Representatives.

R. H. SNYDER,
Lieutenant Governor and President of the Senate.

Approved July 14, 1898.

MURPHY J. FOSTER,
Governor of the State of Louisiana.

A true copy:
JOHN T. MICHEL,
Secretary of State.

INSTITUTE FOR THE DEAF AND DUMB.

Act No. 166.]

AN ACT

To re-organize, establish and maintain the Institution for the Deaf and Dumb, to be known as the "Louisiana Institute for the Deaf and Dumb;" to locate same at Baton Rouge; to provide for the organization and government thereof; to provide for the appointment of a Board of Trustees; to confer corporate powers on said board: to define its powers and duties and to provide for the expense of the members; to define the class of persons to be admitted in the institution, and to prescribe the benefits and privileges they shall receive.

Section 1. Be it enacted by the General Assembly of the State of Louisiana, That there shall be established and maintained, in the town of Baton Rouge, an institution for the education of the deaf and dumb, to be known as the "Louisiana Institute for the Deaf and Dumb."

Sec. 2. Be it further enacted, etc., That the Governor shall appoint, by and with the advice and consent of the Senate, seven resident citizens of the State, together with the Governor, (who shall be ex-officio president of the board) shall constitute and be known as the Board of Trustees of the Louisiana Institute for the Deaf and Dumb. At the first appointment of the board under this act two of the members shall be appointed for two years, two for three years, and three for four years, and thereafter appointments shall be made for the term of four years.

Sec. 3. Be it further enacted, etc., That the Board of Trustees is hereby declared and constituted a body politic corporate, and shall have full power to sue and be sued, to make contracts, and acquire and hold, by purcahse or donation any real or personal property necessary for the use or for the benfit of said institution.

Sec. 4. Be it furthen enacted, etc., That the domicile of the Board of Trustees shall be at Baton Rouge and all process shall be served on the vice-president at the office of the board

Sec. 5. Be it further enacted, etc., That they shall receive, instruct and support in the Institution all persons deaf and dumb, or of such defective speech or haring as not to be able to acquire an education in the ordinary schools, between the ages of eight and twenty-two years, of sound mind and proper health of body, and residents of the State. Such persons shall receive instruction and be provided with boad, lodging, medicine and medical attendance at the expense of the Institution, and if in such indigent circumstances as to render it necessary, shall also be furnished with clothing and traveling expenses to and from the Institution, upon a certificate to that effce from the president of the Police Jury of the parish, or the mayor of the city, or town, in which they reside.

Sec. 7. Be it further enacted, etc., That the persons ad: mitted as pupils under fourteen years of age, may continue in the institution ten years; if over fourteen and under seventeen yars of age, they may continue eight years; if over seventeen years of age, they may continue five years; provided, the board may in any case extend the term two years.

Sec. 8. Be it further enacted, etc., That the first meeting of the Board of Trustees shall be held at such time as the Governor shall direct, and at such meeting they shall elect a vice-president, they shall elect a treasurer, a superintendent and such other officers as may be necessary for the proper organization and management of the Institution, define their duties and fix their salaries.

Sec. 9. Be it further enacted, etc., That the vice-president shall preside over the meetings of the board during the absence of the president, and shall exercise a general supervision over the affairs of the Institution.

Sec. 10. Be it further enacted, etc., That the treasurer shall give bond in such sum as the Board of Trustees may determine, with security to be approved by the vice-president. He shall be custodian of the funds of the Institution. He shall receive from the State Treasurer the monies appropriated by the State for the support of the Institution upon his warrant countersigned by the Governor. He shall make payments upon the order of the Superintendent of the Institute cuntersigned by the vice-president of the board.

Sec. 11. Be it further enacted, etc., That the members of the Board of Trustees shall be paid their expenses incurred in attending the meeting of the board, out of the funds of the Institute.

Sec.12. Be it further enacted, etc., That the Institution shall provide all the requisite facilities for acquiring a good literary education instruction in hygiene and physical culture and an industrial department in which instruction shall be given in such trades as may be best suited to render the pupils self-sustaining citizens.

Sec. 13. Be it further enacted, etc., That upon appointment of the Board of Trustees herein provided for the organization of the Institute for the Deaf and Dumb, at Baton Rouge, under existing laws shall cease and determine, and the new board shall assume custody, management and control thereof.

Sec. 14. Be it further enacted, etc., That this act shall take effect from and after its passage.

S. P. HENRY,
Speaker of the House of Representatives.
R. H. SNYDER,
Lieutenant Governor and President of the Senate.
Approved July 14, 1898.
MURPHY J. FOSTER,
Governor of the State of Louisiana.
A true copy:
JOHN T. MICHEL,
Secretary of State.

SALE FOR THE UNIVERSITY.

Act No. 56.]

AN ACT

Authorizing the Governor to sell certain property of the State, situated in the city of Baton Rouge, at public or private sale, and prescribing the use to be made of the proceeds of said sale.

Whereas, By House Concurrent Resolution No. 16 of 1896, the Governor was authorized to sell certain property of the State, situated in the city of Baton Rouge at a minimum price of twenty thousand dollars ($20,000) and

Whereas, By Act No. 38 of 1896, an appropriation was made to the Louisiana State University and A. and M. College of twenty thousand dollars ($20,000) for the purpose of erecting a building for class and laboratory purposes, said sum to be paid out of the proceeds of the sale of said property, and

Whereas, the Governor of Louisiana has been unable to dispose of said property for the price specified, and the State University has in consequence been unable to draw said appropriation or any portion thereof; therefore,

Section 1. Be it enacted by the General Assembly of the State of Louisiana, That the Governor of the State of Louisiana be and is hereby authorized to sell the said property of the State situated in the city of Baton Rouge in the square bounded by Church, Laurel, Florida and Third streets, and formerly occupied by the Institute for the Deaf and Dumb, to the highest bidder at public or private sale; the terms of said sale to be fixed by the Governor at not less than fifteen thousand ($15,000.00) Dollars, the payment of the balance of said purchase money to be secured by the usual vendor's privilege and mortgage.

Sec. 2. Be it further enacted, that the proceeds of said sale be and the same are hereby appropriated to the Louisiana

State University and Agricultural and Mechanical College for the erection of one or more buildings for class and laboratory purposes.

S. P. HENRY,
Speaker of the House of Representatives.

R. H. SNYDER,
Lieutenant Governor and President of the Senate.

Approved July 8th, 1898.

MURPHY J. FOSTER,
Governor of the State of Louisiana.

A true copy:
JOHN T. MICHEL,
Secretary of State..

RESOLUTIONS AND RULINGS BY THE STATE BOARD OF EDUCATION.

1. (Compulsory Examinations.)—Resolved, that while it is the sense of this board that the provisions contained in Section 50 of Act 81 of 1888 are still in force, that none the less the Parish Superintendent has the right of requiring teachers whom he deems incompetent and inefficient and whom he has the power to remove under the 46th section of said act, to be examined with a view of testing their qualifications and fitness. April 1, 1891.

2. (Examination Schedule.)—1st. Resolved, by the State Board of Education, that the examination of teachers in the several parishes of the State be held hereafter at the time of the regular quarterly meetings of the parish school boards, and at no other time except as hereinafter provided.

2nd. That due notice of the time set for examination of teachers be given by the parish superintendent, also notice that no other examination will be held until the next quarterly meeting of the parish board.

3rd. That the State Superintendent of Education prepare a set of questions covering all the subjects required by law, and furnish to the superintendent of each parish, a sufficient number of copies of these official question lists for use in the examinations, and that no other questions shall be used in said examinations; said questions to be sent out from the superintendent's office so as to reach the several parishes simultaneously, and to be used only once, and only on the dates named above.

4th. That the value of each question be indicated by the State Superintendent, and that a list of answers showing what would be a fair amount of information to be elicited by each question, be prepared by the superintendent and furnished to the examining board of each parish board, for the purpose of establishing a uniform value to the certificates granted in each parish.

5th. That the same question lists be used in examinations of teachers for all grades of certificates, the several grades of certificates being graded according to the percentages made by the candidates.

6th. That the superintendent of each parish furnish to the State Superintendent within two weeks after each examination, a list of all persons examined, with their post office addresses, the grade received and the grade of certificate granted to each candidate.

N. B.—It has been considered proper not to adhere in this examination to instruction in 5th rule.

Examiners will please mark each answer on the scale of 10 for perfect.—August 20, 1896.

3. (High Schools.)—Resolved, That the State Board of Education call the attention of the parish boards to the necessity of establishing high schools wherever the grade of students justifies it, as the State Board of Education believe that the establishment of a number of high schools in the State will contribute powerfully to build up both the public school system and colleges and universities. August 19, 1892.

4. (Collection of Poll Tax.)—The State Board urge the parish school boards to insist upon a full and complete collection of the poll tax, and upon failure of the sheriffs to report as the law directs that suits be instituted against the tax collector for entire amount of the roll as the law directs in Sections 2 and 3 of Act 89, approved July 2nd, 1888. August 19, 1892.

5. (Normal and Other Graduates.)—That the several parish school boards, committees on teachers, and parish superintendents throughout the State are urged to use their best endeavors to secure the services of competent teachers; that many graduates of our State Normal School and of other colleges entitled to a preference in the employment of teachers, desire positions in our schools, many of whom have applied to our State Superintendent for employment, who will furnish their names and addresses on application, and we urge the local authorities to secure the services of such teachers as the best means of advancing the educational interest of the children of the State. August 19, 1892.

6. (Penalty for not Recognizing Normal Graduates.)— Resolved, That the State Superintendent of Public Education be and is hereby ordered and directed to report to the Governor any school boards or members of school boards who fail to give preference to graduates of the State Normal School or other schools and colleges of good standing as di-

rected by resolution of this board passed August 19, 1892, or who fail to remove their parish superintendents who are inefficient, unfaithful, or negligent in the discharge of their duties, and the Governor is hereby requested to remove such boards or members, subject to the ratification of this board as provided by Section 2 of Act 29, of 1892. October 19, 1892.

7. (Decision in Favor of Normal Graduates.)—Whereas, information has reached this board of the violation by the school board of the parish of Bossier of the resolution adopted by this board of date August 19, 1892, passed in pursuance of Section 9 of Act No. 73 of 1892, exempting Normal graduates from examination and entitling them to a certain degree of preference, therefore

Be it resolved, That the State Superintendent of Public Education be and he is hereby required to notify said parish board of its violation of the said act as well as the resolutions of this board, and in the event of their failure to at once comply with the law and the resolutions of this body that the Govenor be and is hereby requested to remove said board. June 29, 1897.

8. (Neglect of Duty to be reported.)—Resolved, That it is necessary that the parish school boards and the parish school superintendents shall rigidly adhere to the laws governing the public schools, and where any neglect or violation by any member of any board, or any neglect or violation of law by any parish superintendent, of any of provisions of such public school laws, shall come to the knowledge of the State Superintendent of Public Education, he shall at once report the facts to the Governor of the State, with the request that he remove such delinquent under the provisions of section 2 of Act 29 of 1892 amending and re-enacting Section 8 of Act 81 of 1888. October 19, 1894.

9. (Uniformity of Text Books.)—Whereas, the law provides under Section 3rd, of Act 81 of 1888 that a uniform series of text books shall be used in the public schools, and

Whereas this requirement has the merit of system and is in line with strict economy, and its wisdom has been thoroughly established by experience, therefore

Be it resolved, That it shall be the duty of the superintendents in the several parishes to see that this rule is faithfully enforced and that the text books adopted or recommended by this board, and none others, are used in the public schools throughout the State.

Resolved Further, That a breach of the law requiring the use of uniform text books as above stated, after notice by the parish superintendent, shall be deemed sufficient grounds for the summary dismissal of any teacher in the public schools. June 29, 1897.

10. Regulating the Price of School Books.)—Whereas, complaint has been made that some of the local dealers in school books in the country have been charging more than the contract prices for text books selected for use in the public schools, therefore

Be it Resolved, That it shall be the duty of the parish superintendents in the several parishes to post in a conspicious place in the school rooms printed schedules of prices at which it has been agreed to furnish the books, and the patrons of the schools shall be notified by him that they can be obtained from the publishers through the the parish superintendents, for cash, at these prices, in case any additional charges are made by local dealers.

Resolved Further, That the State Superintendent of Public Education shall forward to the parish superintendents these printed price lists.

11. (Regulating Sale of School Books.)—Be it Resolved, That the Depositaries appointed by this board are prohibited from in any way invalidating by their actions the contracts entered into by the board and the several publishing houses. October 19, 1894.